Welcome
to the
Mardi Gra Experience

Welcome to the Mardi Gra Experience

by
Simon Cooper

BLAKE

Published by Blake Publishing Ltd,
3 Bramber Court, 2 Bramber Road,
London W14 9PB, England

First published in 1999

ISBN 1 85782 3516

British Library Cataloguing-in-Publication Data:
A catalogue record for this book is available
from the British Library.

Typeset by T2

Printed in Great Britain by
Creative Print and Design (Wales),
Ebbw Vale, Gwent.

1 3 5 7 9 10 8 6 4 2

Pictures reproduced by kind permission of The Metropolitan
Police Service and PA News.

For Sarah

'Te amo'

Acknowledgements

Firstly, a large round of thanks to John Blake, Adam, Charly, Rosie and everyone at Blake Publishing for their support and for putting up with me. Thank you Ian Stephen, for the loan of your mind. Thank you Keith Bray, Dr Chris Side, Frank Swann, Graeme McLagan, Roy Ramm and everyone who contributed their knowledge, time and enthusiasm to this project. Special thanks to those people whom I cannot publicly name. Thank you John O'Connor for some of the best boozy afternoons I can't remember. Thank you Julian Cooper for taking a photograph of me for this book's jacket that actually makes me look human. Thank you Ben Timberlake, for the loan of your camera and the great oysters. And thank you Bob Duffield, my good friend, confidant, supporter and all-round guardian angel. Sarah — what can I say? 'Thank you' seems such an inadequate phrase to express my feelings for all the support you have given me. Nevertheless — THANK YOU. Last, but by no means least, thank you, thank you, thank you Mum and Dad, for your unquestioning love and support.

Contents

How many of our daydreams would darken into nightmares if there seemed any danger of their coming true?

Logan Pearsall Smith, *Afterthoughts*

Author's Note
Edgar Pearce, Ronald Pearce and their families refused to
co-operate with the writing of this book.

July 2, 1998

Welcome to the Mardi Gra Experience

There they were.

They stood, heads slightly bowed, flanked by three prison officers. Outside the dock, a small huddle of the court's private security guards lurked.

These were the Mardi Gra bombers?

All around them, the chaos of Horseferry Road Magistrates Court continues without pause, almost as though they aren't there. Nothing interrupts its pace. Was this the recognition they'd sought for so long? Clerks and ushers ferry to and fro, lawyers queue and shuffle at the back of the court, conferring in too-loud whispers that echo up to the ceiling, waiting their turn as a continual stream of unfortunates, degenerates and lost souls take a place in the dock to answer to society.

The Stipendary Magistrate, Mr Timothy Workman

efficiently clears away the drunk and disorderlies, the overnight remands, the wife beater, the psychiatric patient, hopelessly lost amid the hustle and bustle.

And then numbers 25 and 26 on Mr Workman's list appear. Edgar Eugene Pearce and Ronald Russell Pearce. They are both dressed in greens — a dark green sweatshirt for Edgar, a light green granddad shirt for Ronald. They are quiet. They still don't seem to quite believe they have reached this point in their lives.

Mr Workman barely lifts his head from the papers before him. Just another two to process. He looks like a severe bank manager, grey suit, grey hair, grey face. This is a routine remand and it is over quickly. The brothers must return to their prisons for another 28 days.

They are led away. They say nothing, look at no one. Not even each other. Before they are out of the door that leads to the holding cells, their place in the dock is being taken by another.

Mr Workman lifts his head.

The court whirls before him.

The door closes. They are gone.

Let the Madness Begin

'He had created a masterpiece. He thought it quite beautiful.

It sat on the workbench of the man's shed, all wrapped up and ready to go. This was going to be good. This would make them take notice.

He began to tidy up, putting the components neatly away — the metal tubes, the springs and wires. Lastly, he returned the half-empty box of shotgun cartridges to its hiding place. After all, he didn't want any accidents happening.

Not today. Because today was the day.

It was time to party.

In the end, the money ceased to matter for him. The winning was all that counted. It had begun as a way of getting even — legitimate and justifiable because after all, for too long he had been done down. By life, by fate, by everything and everyone. No longer. After months of thinking and planning he'd thought up a way of making things right again. Actually, he'd been shown a way. He'd seen it in the light that glowed in the corner of the room from the television he rarely switched off.

He had seen it and he had acted upon it. He had channelled his hate and made something creative out of it. He'd let his bitterness fail him for too long. Now he had turned it to a strength that few others could understand.

And this time he had to win. He couldn't fail. Not again.

Dear God, he couldn't fail again.

On the morning of December 6, 1994 six parcels were delivered to six different addresses in London. The madness was about to begin. It was a madness that would stretch over three and-a-half years, cost an estimated £10 million, tie the police in knots and culminate in one of the largest police operations ever mounted in Britain.

Martin Grimsdale, a clerk at Barclays Bank, Ladbroke Grove branch, was sorting through the post as he always did first thing. Nestled amongst the dozens of letters and packages was an item which was — well, odd.

It was a parcel, about the size of a book, wrapped in cheery blue Christmas paper decorated with myriad gold snowflakes. The address had been typed on a home-made label by an old-fashioned typewriter. The first class stamp was franked as being sorted at 5.13 p.m. the previous day. All pretty straightforward. The odd thing was in the bottom left-hand corner of the label: a photocopied picture of four men in suits and ties. It looked for all the world as though it were a still from Reservoir Dogs. Underneath the picture were the words:

WELCOME TO THE

MARDI GRA EXPERIENCE

Martin turned the parcel over in his hands. Who'd send their bank manager a Christmas present? Maybe someone desperate for a festive loan. His fingers began to pull at the blue festive tape securing the wrapping paper.

Several miles away in Hampstead, staff at Barclays High Street branch were reeling. At 8.27 a.m., a Christmas present delivered with the morning mail had blown up as it

6

was being opened by Bali Hari, a part-time clerk. As staff were dialling the police and evacuating the building . . .

Martin pulled the last of the tape free and ripped the paper off the package.

It was a video. And in the sleeve was that same four-man picture and the same strange, sinister greeting.

WELCOME TO THE

MARDI GRA EXPERIENCE

It was 8.31 a.m.

As Martin lifted the cover of the video case, a small metal catch inside slipped from its anchor, releasing a tightly compressed spring. In a split second the spring had powered a home-made firing pin onto the base of a shotgun cartridge.

The case exploded in Martin's hands. There was a loud bang and a blinding flash. The smell of burning, acrid smoke filled the room.

Five minutes later in King Street, Hammersmith, an identical parcel to the two at Hampstead and Ladbroke Grove was discovered. By then, Barclays security staff had sounded the warning, calling each branch in a desperate bid to halt the opening of the morning's post. The message was soon flashing around London — look out for Christmas presents in the post. Look out for gold snow flakes. Look out for the Mardi Gra Experience. Police sealed off Hammersmith and the two branches where the explosions had occurred. Officers from Scotland Yard's Anti Terrorist Branch (SO13) were called out and quickly arrived at Hammersmith. Donning their distinctive green protective clothing, they entered the bank. More phone calls began to arrive at Scotland Yard's central operations room. More presents had been found in the post at Barclays branches all over west London. More SO13 teams were sent out.

09.15: Barclays Bank, Gloucester Road, W8 — SO13 recovered another package.

09.30: Barclays Bank, Kensington High Street, W8 —
SO13 officers carried out a controlled explosion on a
suspect package.

11.42: Barclays Bank, Edgware Road, NW9 — another
deadly present was made safe by explosives officers.

That parcel was to be the last that day.

As soon as the word 'bomb' had been heard on the 999
calls received that morning, primary command of the police
operation devolved to SO13. Even though the IRA had
announced a total cessation of violence just four months
previously, the police and security services were still on a
state of high preparedness. Could the Barclays explosions be
the start of a new terror campaign? Those cynical of the
IRA's motives, suspecting the ceasefire was nothing more
than a mask for a regrouping exercise, had been warning
there would be more attacks, as sure as night follows day.

However, when the bomb squad officers arrived at the
scenes of the attacks, they quickly ruled out IRA
involvement; in fact, the involvement of any mainstream
terrorist group seemed highly unlikely. As one officer on the
case stated, 'The target was wrong, the technology of the
device was wrong; it was kitchen table stuff.'

And of course, there was the seasonal packaging and
that strange logo.

With SO13 quickly ruling out a terrorist attack, a
major criminal investigation was launched under the control
of Roy Ramm, commander of the Metropolitan Police's
Specialist Operations (SO) department. SO is to the Met
what the SAS is to the Army. It is made up of a cadre of
highly experienced officers who work both for the Met as
their regional force and nationally. With a Met assistant
commissioner as its head, SO is run on a day-to-day basis by
a commander level officer — in this case Roy Ramm. SO is
split into five groups; Crime, Intelligence, Protection,
Security and Identification, with each group in turn split
into sub-groups of specialist teams.

It was to the officers from the SO's Hostage and Extortion Unit that initial responsibility for investigating the Mardi Gra Experience was to fall. They weren't to know then how long it would take to close the curtain on the experience or down how many blind alleys they would be led. It was just a matter of getting on with the job.

After all the scenes were secured, officers began to recover what evidence there was. With six sites scattered across the west of the city, Organised Crime put 50 officers on to the case immediately. It was essential to quickly ensure that the crime scenes weren't contaminated. As Ramm said, 'We didn't want people walking away with the evidence. And with bomb attacks, people can literally walk away with the evidence stuck in the ridges on the soles of their shoes. The sites were sealed off to the public and staff, statements were taken and security videos seized.'

Three devices had been recovered intact, two had exploded, and one had been detonated by SO13. The bombs had been concealed inside double-sized video cases and were clearly home made. The 'bomb' was in fact a spring-loaded bolt with a nail fixed to one end. Fastened onto the end of the device was a shotgun cartridge primed with firework gunpowder and loaded with ball bearings. The fact that it was such an amateur effort saved Martin and Bali from serious injury. The pellets had been packed too loosely in the cartridge sleeve, so when the bolt slammed onto the base of the cartridge, they did not explode out as the attacker had intended. However, the gunpowder explosion left Martin suffering from temporary deafness and Bali with burns to her hands and face. A forensic expert was later to say that if the cartridges had been fully viable, they could easily have killed their targets.

All major police investigations are given an operational name. The names are selected at random by a computer. The computer chose Operation Heath for the Mardi Gra investigation. The first line of enquiry for Operation Heath was to try and find out where the bomb's components had come from. If the video cases, bolts or cartridge shells were from a limited line of production or had restricted distribution, it would quickly narrow down the field of suspects to those who had access to such materials. The method of construction could also yield vital clues. By looking at the techniques used by Mardi Gra, scientists might be able to establish if the bomber was someone with a background in electronics or maybe some sort of mechanic or engineer.

Other teams were tasked with combing through Barclays personnel records and customer complaint files. The most likely culprit in any attack against a commercial organisation is going to be either a dissatisfied customer or a disgruntled ex-member or current member of staff. Detectives, aided by Barclays, would have to wade through thousands of pages of records and correspondence to try and identify anyone who might have built up a deadly grudge over the years. Yet more detectives would spend hours combing police records of known blackmailers.

Finally, there was the cryptic packaging. What did it all mean? Was there a message contained in the wording or the picture? Why would someone go to all that trouble to create such an unusual combination of slogan and image? One of the most obvious features of the wording was the spelling mistake — 'Gra' instead of 'Gras'. If there was a hidden message, and they could crack it, it could lead the straight to the culprit's door. Was it some kind of anagram or a cryptic message. Maybe someone who fancied themselves as a master criminal, aspiring to the high wit of 'The Penguin'?

Despite all the unknowns at this early stage, there were things the team could do immediately to narrow the gap between themselves and the bomber. With everyone in agreement that this was the opening shot of an extortion campaign a tactical decision needed to be taken about publicising the attacks. It was a decision that could potentially shape the way the entire case evolved.

If the bomber fitted the regular extortionist profile, Roy Ramm knew from experience that he or she would be very unlikely to do anything where they were putting themselves personally at risk. 'They are not prepared to run across the road into a building society and shove a gun up someone's nose. It doesn't make them nicer criminals, says Ramm, 'they just don't have the courage for face-to-face crime.'

Back in the 1970s Ramm had done a lot of profiling in this area. Generally, he says, extortionists have little or no criminal background. A lot of extortionists will say: 'I'll tell you how this started. I was skint. I was playing on the computer, I was playing around, it was almost going to be a story, it was a plot, then I didn't do anything for a month and then the gas bill came and the electricity bill came and I thought "fuck it, I'll do it, I'll take this show on the road." '

Unlike professional criminals, blackmailers generally don't have a support network. Ramm says, 'most career criminals have people who work in the same area, people they can rely on, particularly if things go wrong. They have an infrastructure of support. The extortionist, by contrast, is operating alone in virgin territory. They have no fall-back position, so they try to work the crime out very carefully stage by stage, literally saying, "this is what will happen, this is what I'll do next." ' So as soon as Ramm saw the nature of the devices sent to Barclays he knew that a demand would arrive soon after.

The extortionist had his plan. What Ramm's team had to do was nudge him off it. But not too hard, because that could annoy him and push him into something really destructive. They just had to alter his game plan enough to make him think on his feet. Ramm explains, 'If he had to start thinking in real time, then he'd be more likely to start making mistakes because of his basic criminal naivety'.

One way to try and force extortionists to make a mistake is to keep them in the dark about the effects of their campaign. This is done by enforcing a news blackout. But the pros and cons of taking such a course of action are finely balanced between the safety of the public and the needs of the investigation. Was there anything to gain by going public at this stage? Somebody might know who was doing it, but the chances were extremely low because of the profile of whoever was responsible. The extortionist was almost certainly a loner — the whole nature of the crime was a secretive thing. Furthermore, whatever the extortionist sends through the post is often the extent of their threat. They might claim they can do more, but they want to stay hidden and that limits their actions. By involving the media, the risk was that the investigating team would give the initial incident greater weight and feed the bombers sense of self-importance. The last thing they wanted to do was encourage him. By keeping news of what had happened controlled, however, the extortionist had no way of knowing whether his plan was working or not.

There was another factor. Going public could damage Barclays irreparably, and most likely for no gain. Roy Ramm gives this analogy, 'Whenever I've lectured to companies on the investigation of extortion, I tell the story of the farmer whose got problems with one fox who eats one chicken once a month. Then along comes the hunt with 50 horses. They catch the fox, but they flatten all the crops. The cure is far worse than the problem. We felt that the potential harm to Barclays was quite disproportionate to the threat at that stage. So we were quite content that on balance there was nothing to achieve from going public.'

So the team had to play a waiting game. If this was the extortion they thought it was, a demand was bound to follow. As it turned out they wouldnt have to wait long for Mardi Gra to get in touch. Two days later on December 8, Mardi Gra declared his hand. The letter was typed and carried the four-man Mardi Gra logo with the banner, 'Welcome to the Mardi Gra Experience'.

Mardi Gra was forthright. His letter demanded, '£2,000 per day, 365 days per annum . . . in the event of a negative response all Barclays staff will be regarded as dispensable targets'.

It went on to detail the method of payment and the means of communication to be used. Mardi Gra wanted Barclays to produce promotional Barclaycards which were to be given away in magazines. The cards would look like dummy Barclaycards but would actually contain a magnetic strip on the back enabling them to be used as cashcards. Only Mardi Gra would have the PIN number which could activate the cards and this would be given to him via a message in the personal column of the Daily Telegraph. The letter was signed 'Mardine Graham' — MARDIine GRAham — another obvious piece of word play from the bomber.

So Mardi Gra had put his cards on the table. The police now knew what they were faced with and at least a little of what the extortionist was capable of. What they didn't know was just how far Mardi Gra was prepared to go to get what he wanted. What they weren't to know until the moment of arrest years later, was why he had embarked on such a vicious campaign.

The answer to that mystery lay behind the door of a modest house in a quiet suburb of London just a few miles from the frenetic activity taking place at New Scotland Yard.

A Useful Handyman

Welcome to the Mardi Gra Experience

He was a quiet, gentle man. He was someone who mocked a man dying of cancer.

He was a reptile.

He wasn't screwed up. He was a weird recluse.

He was revolted by racial prejudice, particularly apartheid. Yet he hated gays and students.

He was a depressive alcoholic who shunned his neighbours and terrorised the local children. He was, to quote another neighbour, a useful handyman — the man to ask if you needed your kettle mended or wanted to know something about wine, politics or just the world at large. In the mêlée following Edgar Pearce's arrest and subsequent conviction, a confusing and contradictory picture of the man who eventually admitted being the Mardi Gra bomber emerged.

Depending on who you talked to, you got a different picture.

One of his neighbours, Kim Thomas, said in an interview with the *Daily Mail*, 'He was never friendly to anyone. If schoolchildren came near his property, he would shout at them to go away. Once, when I walked past with my dogs and they strayed on to his patch of grass at the front, he shouted, "Get them away or I'll poison them." '

To Breda Williams, another neighbour, Pearce was simply, 'Weird. He wouldn't speak to anyone at all.'

Terry O'Neill lived two doors away from Pearce. He describes a kinder version of the man the Sun dubbed the 'Mardi Gra Monster' According to Terry, Pearce was a man who could talk about anything and turn his hand to anything practical. If anyone wanted anything done, he was the man to ask. 'But I always felt he was frustrated intellectually.' His wife Frances agrees, 'He was very intelligent, very artistic with his hands, very creative.'

Another neighbour concurred, telling the *Daily Mail*, 'He could turn his hand to anything. He was always tinkering in the house or in the shed. He always seemed a bit unsatisfied . . . a bit of a Van Gogh, a frustrated character — he was so talented but it was difficult for him to use his talent.'

Pearce's talent. His intelligence. His meticulous nature.

These are the character traits which marked him out from the rest of the crowd during his life before he came to be the Mardi Gra bomber. And those same traits became part of his arsenal when he began to construct and then activate his plan for blackmail.

But until police walked in through the door of 12, Cambridge Road North in Chiswick, at just past 1 a.m. on the morning of April 29, all the outside world really knew about Pearce was that he was simply another man approaching his pension years, living an outwardly nondescript life in a nondescript cul-de-sac, in a nondescript area of west London

Edgar Eugene Pearce was born in east London on August 7, 1937. He was named after his father, Edgar Russell Pearce, a tailor who worked as a gentleman's outfitter. Almost six years earlier, Edgar senior and his wife Constance had had their first child Ronald. The family was to be completed several years later with the birth of a third son, Phillip.

The Pearce's were a traditional family. While dad went out to work, mother Constance stayed at home to look after the children. As the boys grew up, Ronald seemed quite content to follow his father into the rag trade, eventually becoming a clothes designer. But young Edgar was a bright lad. At the age of eleven he was sent to Nelson House, a preparatory school in Oxford. Sending Edgar to this fee-paying school required huge sacrifices for the rest of the family. But they felt it would be worthwhile. Edgar carried with him all their hopes for the future, the chance for their son to make something of himself, the chance for the family name to be respected outside their tight-knit working class community.

And it was here that a pattern was to set in Pearce's life that would repeat itself numerous times over the years; a pattern made up of disappointments, lost opportunities and frustrated ambition and with each repetition of this cycle, his resentment of the world grew.

Three years after he started at his prep school, the dream of private education was over. His father, always struggling to afford the prohibitive costs, finally bowed to the inevitable and told his son that he'd have to leave. Pearce returned to Leyton, and was sent to the local school, Norlington Road Boys' School. One can only imagine the young boy's disappointment and, probably anger, at having to come down in the world. But whatever feelings he harboured, he still managed to acquire a respectable education and when he left school at eighteen, Pearce went on to Charing Cross Polytechnic to study advertising. The East End boy was still determined to go up in the world, despite the early set back.

On the February 25, 1961, Pearce married twenty-year-old Maureen Fitzgerald at Surrey Northern Registry Office. On their marriage certificate, Pearce gives his occupation as 'Advertising Executive'. It seems he met his bride through work, as Maureen is described as an Accounts Clerk (Advertising Agency). The newlyweds settled down to begin enjoying life in their new home in East Sheen, south-west London. Edgar was doing well in the advertising business, gaining steady promotion and broadening his experience with several agencies. But in 1971, Pearce and Maureen moved to South Africa. Pearce appears to have got bored with advertising and taken a job as a 'freelance adviser' to a TV production company. He was eternally restless, convinced he wasn't moving up the ladder fast enough. If people in Britain didn't want to see him shine, then maybe South Africa was the place to be.

A year after emigrating, Maureen gave birth to daughter Nicola. Pearce got on with making his way in the world — and began to develop an intense interest in guns. South Africa possesses a very gun oriented culture, stemming heavily from the pioneer spirit of the white settlers, the resulting paranoia spawned by apartheid, and the seemingly inexorable rise in urban violence there. It was normal, you carried a gun, you discussed them with your neighbours and work colleagues like you'd discuss the weather. In this environment, Pearce became intimate with the ins and outs of many kinds of weapon and their ammunition. It was knowledge he brought home when the family decided to return to Britain in 1976.

The move had been looming for some time. South Africa wasn't the new start Pearce had dreamed of. Pearce grew to hate the apartheid system with its clear winners and losers. He was also worried by the tinderbox political situation developing as the black majority became more vocal in their demands for equal rights and the minority white government waged a war of repression against them. The emigration experiment hadn't worked. It was a brave venture that had turned again to dust. Another opportunity not quite grasped.

Back home, Pearce decided to reinvent himself. He had always been a keen chef so he and Maureen decided to set up their own restaurant. They bought a small bistro in Hayling Island, called *Jeanne's Cuisine* and set about their new venture with bright enthusiasm. Pearce, of course, was the chef as well as playing the role of host. He seemed to genuinely enjoy his new way of life. After his conviction, the *Daily Mirror* ran a picture of him in the restaurant. In it, he is rake thin, a far cry from the swollen, pot-bellied man he was to become and whose deeply unflattering mug shot was to be plastered across every paper in the country. In the *Mirror* photograph he is standing attentively next to a table full of happy looking diners, filling a notebook with their orders.

However, as with most things in Pearce's life, things were crumbling under the surface. The restaurant did not do well. The locals blamed it on Pearce's 'fancy' cooking. Here was Pearce again trying to show the world just how much he had to offer, displaying a talent that no one wanted to recognise. Few warmed to the exotic dishes he served up and custom began to drop off.

Pearce started drinking heavily and acting in an 'eccentric' manner. According to one regular, Pearce took to dressing up like a Frenchman in beret and scarf. More disturbingly, he started wandering into the restaurant with a shotgun and is said to have fired it into the ceiling on a number of occasions while the restaurant was full of diners enjoying their evening meals. Whether the drinking and odd behaviour were precipitated by the decline of the business or visa versa is not clear. Either way, by the early 1980s, the bank was refusing to loan the bistro any more to keep it going. Worse was to follow. Maureen became gravely ill with cancer. Unable to run the business on his own, Pearce was forced to sell in 1982, something he desperately wanted to avoid.

The bank that had refused Pearce's pleas for more money was Barclays.

During the course of the forced sale, Pearce managed to delude himself that the manager of his local Barclays branch was in collusion with a local solicitor who was handling the sale. He accused them of trying to drag the proceedings out to hamper the sale and allow the bank to repossess when a buyer couldn't be found. Typical Pearce; blame everybody but yourself. A buyer was found, but Pearce managed to salvage just £5,000 from his dream project. Another bitter failure to add to his tally.

It was back to London for the Pearce family. Another step down the ladder, a ladder he was supposed to be ascending. In the space of a few years he had gone from owning a business and his own home to being unemployed and transient. With only the meagre proceeds from the bistro's sale to live on, Pearce had to rely on the council to house his family when he finally settled in Chiswick, close to his elder brother Ronald. Pearce was allocated a three-bedroom flat in a converted Victorian villa at 12, Cambridge Road North.

Cambridge Road North. A cul-de-sac at the far end of Chiswick, and a drastic come down . . . The phenomenally busy M4 motorway whooshes past one end, a flyover section literally at eye level to the upper floors of the houses there. And, being directly under the Heathrow flight path, jets roar interminably overhead. At the other end of Cambridge Road North lies Chiswick High Road. It's a part of London people pass though to get somewhere else. The air seems permanently thick with the smell of exhaust fumes from idling, impatient engines.

Not a place for people with choice. But at least Ronald lived only fifteen minutes away in a flat he shared with his long-term partner Sonia Bickham.

Pearce reinvented himself again, this time as a property developer. He wasn't a massive success, even through the housing boom of the late eighties, but he did enough to keep body and soul together and the bailiffs away.

That is until 1992.

For Pearce, 1992 was to be the lowest point in a long decline. The worst year in a succession of bad ones. He was still drinking heavily, still not defined in his identity, still smarting over what might have been. The stresses were too much for his marriage. Edgar and Maureen separated, with Maureen leaving the house. Thirty years of marriage were over, just like that.

To finance himself, Pearce began to illegally sub-let the council house. He moved himself into the front room on the ground floor, leaving the three bedrooms on the second floor free for his tenants. With the rooms let out, he was earning around £600–£750 a month, enough to cover the council's rent, pay for the groceries and support his drinking, which if it had been heavy before, now reached staggering levels. Pearce would drink bottle after bottle of red wine or spend all day in the pub before coming home to start yet more drinking; he could easy down a dozen cans of lager at home after a heavy afternoon session at the local.

He was drinking himself to breaking point.

That point arrived in August of the same year when Pearce was found collapsed in the street near his home. On the way to hospital he suffered a fit and continued to fit after his admission. Doctors told him he had developed epilepsy and the fits he had suffered had damaged his brain. Pearce had also broken his shoulder in the fall, an injury so severe, surgery was needed to repair the damage.

When Pearce eventually emerged from hospital he was a changed man — changed in the sense he had finally been pushed over the edge. He was more bitter and angry than ever. His injuries had been so severe, it looked like he would never work again. He came home to a house full of people, but empty of life.

The only option was to retreat to his front room and slam the door on the world. Despite stern warnings from his doctors he went back to the drink in a big way, topping it up with endless painkillers. And when his prescriptions ran out he topped up the pills himself, with strong non-prescription Ibuprofen and Remegel for the acid aches in his gut. He sat in front of the TV for hours on end. 'I had no lifestyle,' he said of that black period. 'My life was TV; all day; all night.'

Although, over time, he recovered physically from his injuries, his behaviour became increasingly bizarre. Ronald's partner Sonia noticed a great personality change after Pearce returned from hospital. He would be up and about at 6 a.m., cooking himself a full roast dinner with all the trimmings. Beef, lamb, duck, venison and quail were all consumed as breakfast, washed down with a bottle of red wine. The fridge would be full of quails' eggs, on which he would gorge whenever it took his fancy. A fluent French speaker, Pearce would take off to France to load up his Vauxhall Senator with cheap wine and lager from the huge hypermarkets near the ferry ports. Lodgers noticed how the car would return almost broken onto its axles, there was so much wine loaded into it. Pearce's favourite tipple was Sicilian wine, which he bought in bulk: boxes piled in a mountain near the door of his room as though there might be a world shortage any day.

His mood and appearance continued to decline, though he tried to keep the charade up with his tenants, sticking to his fantasy that he was still a property developer who owned the £340,000 home. In reality, he was living on disability allowance and renting it from the council for £51.10 a week. He liked his tenants to call him 'Eddie' and tried to make the house as homey as possible, adding little touches like a communal iron, which was mounted on a wall under a notice gently reminding the last user to 'Please replace the iron in its holder after use.' But the nice Eddie who pottered around the house doing odd jobs and keeping the place generally tidy was fighting a losing battle to keep another version of Eddie in check. That other Eddie emerged when Pearce got a drink inside him, but as the years following the accident plodded along, the other Eddie began to appear without the help of the drink.

Graham Hirst lodged with Pearce for two years, and left Cambridge Road North with a low opinion of his landlord, an opinion he shared with the *Sun* following Pearce's conviction. Hirst told the newspaper, 'To him, everyone was worthless, almost beneath him. He was the sort of man who wouldn't bat an eyelid if one of his explosions wiped out an entire family. He was as cold as a reptile, totally and utterly unconcerned about the welfare of anyone else. But he surpassed even himself when talking about his brother-in-law John, who was dying of stomach cancer. He told me, "That man's always whinging. Why doesn't he just get on with it?"

Sue and Mark Hinchcliffe told how Pearce's drinking made him a nightmare to live with. 'He would frequently arrive home blind drunk. He was horrible when he was drunk. He'd lie full length on the stairs and spend hours rambling on the phone.' The Hinchcliffes moved out after three months.

Pearce didn't leave a good impression with his neighbours either. A woman who lived in the basement flat below Pearce's flat told how he made her life hell after she rejected a pass he had made at her while drunk. The woman complained Pearce deliberately flooded her flat and gave her teenage son a live bullet. She went on to find piles of shotgun cartridges by her front door. The acrimony between the neighbours culminated in a fight between Pearce and the woman's husband, which left Pearce sprawled on the floor and needing hospital treatment for a fractured jaw.

Graham Hirst adds this revealing comment about the state Pearce had got himself into. 'When neighbours passed him in the street, he wouldn't acknowledge them. Mind you, few people thought much of him either. He only got one Christmas card — in childish handwriting without any love or kisses.'

No love or kisses. Just the drink to fall back on and the anger to keep him going.

1994. Nearly two years had passed since his accident. Yet Pearce still sat slumped in his sofa, a thick toothache throb knawing away in his smashed shoulder. In a fug of painkillers and alcohol, the television became his mirror on the world. But it also taunted him. It took him on holiday to all the places he'd never been, let him glimpse the lifestyles he would never enjoy. It showed him how good life could be and how bad his own was. He wallowed ever deeper, took more pills and more wine.

Then one day, the television showed him something so fantastic, so remarkable, he could hardly believe it. It pulled him off the sofa and out from under the smothering cloak of his depression. It showed him a way to turn things round, how to bring all the good things out there into his life.

Best of all, it showed him how he was going to show them.

It was his epiphany.

He was better than all of them put together. Life had dealt him a bad hand to date. But he was about to become the dealer.

He wasn't a failure. His time just hadn't come yet.

Well, it was coming now.

He'd been looking for something, an image, a way of making sure they knew he was responsible.

It would be like going back to the old days, back to advertising. Except this campaign would be his very own -- no interfering no-brains telling him how they could improve his ideas simply because they were higher up the brown-nosing ladder.

He'd show them by using a very basic principle of advertising:

convince people of what you want to do by a plan that is consistent and persuasive. Well, things didn't get much more persuasive than this.

Branding was the key to the whole thing. You had to have a brand. He'd got his slogan. This was going to be 'The Mardi Gras Experience', but Mardi Gras with a little twist of his own — Mardi Gras without the 's'. He knew that would mark everything he did as his. He also knew the spelling mistake would keep the police guessing forever. And while they were off chasing ghosts, he could start making some — with bombs.

But he needed an image — you can't have an advertising campaign without a 'look'. He sat in front of the television brooding over it, flicking through Home Entertainment magazines, catalogues, books on every subject under the sun. Then finally, there it was, staring him right in the face. Four guys dressed up like the Blues Brothers. Or was it Reservoir Dogs? It didn't matter. The image was perfect, all threatening and stylish and intriguing.

He went to work, cutting and pasting the image and the slogan together. A few hours spent photocopying at the local library and leafing through their phone books completed the mission. He was ready to start his campaign.

For the first time in years, he whistled as he made his way home.

Anytime, Anyplace ... Anyone

Welcome to the Mardi Gra Experience

With six bombs delivered on one day, Mardi Gra had shown he meant business. There seemed to be nothing to lose by trying to open a line of communication with him. As instructed, the Met placed an advert in the *Daily Telegraph*'s personals column on December 10. In amongst the love messages and thanks to St Jude, the following appeared:

O.K. MARDINE GRAHAM, sorry was late, I was confused. Please explain. Richard.

It drew no response. Mardi Gra had sent a demand note then gone to ground, ignoring the message he had specifically asked for. Not for the last time, Pearce would simply drop away, leaving his targets and the police frustrated, nervous and enduring an uncomfortable wait until the next time Mardi Gra decided to announce his presence.

1995 dawned. January turned to February and still there was no sign or communication from Mardi Gra. Meanwhile, banking matters of a different kind held the country's attention. In Singapore, rogue trader Nick Leeson had run up losses of £850 million, and brought down one of Britain's oldest established financial institutions, Barings bank.

Three more months ticked by.

During this time information from the lines of enquiry set up in the immediate aftermath of the explosions was continuing to trickle in. Unfortunately, the news which was coming back was mostly negative. Dozens of detectives had been sent out to try and discover the origin of the video cases and the bolts used in the firing mechanisms. Endless manufacturers, retailers and industry experts were contacted and interviewed, but to no avail. The components were all terribly ordinary. Anyone could have bought them from just about anywhere in the country.

There was little for forensics to go on either. The bomber had clearly gone to great lengths to avoid leaving thumbprints, hairs or any revealing debris on his devices. All that could be gleaned for certain was the pretty obvious. Here was a man who, although obviously amateur, was an accomplished handyman with a good understanding of how mechanical and electrical things worked.

Then there was what is known as the 'victimology' — the study of who the victim is and why anyone would want to attack them. Roy Ramm explains, 'Although there is a demand and the underlying motive is money, you are nevertheless compelled to ask 'why Barclays and not Lloyds or the Midland?' There might still be 'the arsehole factor' —

someone's got the hump about something that just happens to drive them towards a particular victim. You get they guy who says 'I was skint, I had no money, I lost my job because Barclays called in the loan on the company I worked for.' They might decide to go for the specific bank which called in the loan or to go for banks generally. What drives them to be able to justify what they are doing could literally be anything and trying to identify that from paper records is almost impossible.'

However, most of the victimology work was directed at trying to identify dissatisfied Barclays customers and members of staff. The task was enormous. Countless hours were spent with senior security people at Barclays, discussing, investigating and rejecting potential threats. But with such a huge organisation, the job of discounting everybody connected with it was close to impossible.

Barclays current files were the first line of attack, then the team had to start going further back into the archives, reading and assessing, making judgements about the level of acrimony involved in customer complaints letters, financial disputes, legal wranglings — anything severe enough, or odd enough to stick out. But the problem was that the process couldn't help but be subjective; what was a deadly trigger to one person might be a minor annoyance to another. Extortionists don't show their hand until they have to. It could be anybody.

To exacerbate the search, Barclays had themselves created a large list of 500 disgruntled people — their own staff. In 1993, the bank had been in the middle of a large voluntary redundancy programme aimed at removing thousands of workers from its books. But as volunteers for redundancy began to drop off, the bank moved in and sacked 500 workers in London and the south east. The move created considerable anger and bitterness among the bank's workforce and the unions threatened strike action. The police had to consider that one of those 500 sacked staff could have decided to mount a strike of a very different kind to get their own back on the bank.

One of the lighter tasks to befall the detectives in the case was the job of decoding Mardi Gra's slogan and imagery. Soon every policeman who fancied himself as a crossword solver was fiddling around with anagrams of 'Welcome to the Mardi Gra Experience' trying to detect any hidden message that might be there. It is easy to see how many hours could be absorbed on this task. 'Mardi Gra' on its own generates combinations such as 'rig drama', 'mig raider' and 'raid gram'. 'Mardi Gra Experience' yields gems including 'pig racer re-examined', 'ex-epidemic arranger' and 'expired crane mirage', while 'Welcome to the Mardi Gra Experience' can be re-worked into 'electromagnetic axed whore empire' and 'hex weeping moderate accelerometer.' As can be seen here, this exercise led precisely nowhere.

The four-man image on the front of the box resulted in one team spending an afternoon watching the film The Blues Brothers after one detective came up with the theory that the image could be styled after the film's two central characters. As the film contained a lot of references to crime, maybe the bomber was re-enacting scenes from the movie. Unsurprisingly, that afternoon's movie watching, while pleasant, yielded no new leads.

More fundamentally, there was the name itself — Mardi Gra, and that missing 's'. The literal translation of Mardi Gra is 'Fat Tuesday' and is traditionally used to describe the feast day which marks the start of the Lenten season of fasting. In recent years, Mardi Gras has become synonymous with wild partying and great carnivals, most notably in Rio de Janeiro and New Orleans. French dictionaries note 'Gras' can be spelt 'Gra' and in that form still means 'fat'. But what did it mean in this context? And was 'Mardine Graham' a significant name, or as suspected, just a play on words? One officer speaking to the *Daily Telegraph* gave this honest appraisal, 'We may find there's no rhyme or reason to any of it. It will probably only be when we arrest someone that we will learn the real significance of the missing 's'.'

Ramm and his team were meeting regularly to review the evidence (or lack of it) to date and to brainstorm new strategies. Included in these meetings were a special team from SO10, the Directorate of Intelligence, whose function is to offer advice and analyses of investigation strategies and available evidence. One of the key problems they had to solve was how to lure Mardi Gra into a dialogue. The demand he had made to Barclays was, according to the bank's security staff, not feasible. At the time, the cost of rewriting the cashpoint software to enable Mardi Gra to make withdrawals of the size he demanded would be prohibitive. 'It would be easier to send him a sack of fivers,' commented one officer.

The team needed to communicate this to Mardi Gra, but Mardi Gra had gone incommunicado. Ramm recalls, 'Obviously we wanted to catch the guy, we really wanted to catch the guy, but if he had decided to go away, that would have been no bad thing. What we didn't want was for him to be put on a learning curve.'

But Mardi Gra was on a learning curve. The failure of Barclays to give him what he wanted had obviously puzzled him. Since December he had been reviewing his strategy and building new, more elaborate bombs. On May 15, after five months of silence, a second demand letter was received at Barclaycard's head office in Northampton.

Mardi Gra was back. And this time he had a horrific new tactic.

Frustrated by his lack of progress with Barclays, Pearce dramatically increased the pressure. Rather than directly target Barclays and their customers, he decided to directly attack individuals selected entirely at random. The idea was to put pressure indirectly on Barclays, while at the same time spreading the campaign. Every device was accompanied by some sort of reference to Barclays, usually a piece of paper bearing the words 'With the Compliments of Barclaycard'.

Pearce hoped that Barclays would crumble and give in to his demands because they would be terrified that word would get out that people were being bombed in their own homes because the bank wasn't paying up. There was also an added bonus for Pearce with this strategy. If there were no links between the victims the police would find it impossible to trace who the bomber was by looking for common associates, but they'd still have to try, just in case there was some tenuous connection. The hours spent searching would be huge.

Picking random targets also delivered another stark message to the police. Pearce was saying 'I can take out anyone.' Pearce fed off the power this gave him, watching people get diverted. The police knew this, but could do nothing about it.

But the plan wasn't working exactly as he wanted. The problem was the lack of publicity. He had expected his first attacks to be big news, but the newspapers had been devoid of any mention, the television and radio silent. Pearce wasn't to know that all coverage of the campaign and attacks had been blacked out. Even though the logical side of his brain suspected the police were behind the suppression, he couldn't help interpreting the lack of press coverage as another case of being ignored. It wasn't *enough* for Barclays and the police to know.

People didn't know. People had to know.

So it was back to Chiswick Library for Pearce, where he had originally photocopied his infamous logo. Using the library's stock of telephone directories, he randomly selected one name from the thousands listed. Then back at his house, Pearce mailed a bomb to that first address — the home of an agricultural surveyor in Peterborough. The brown paper package arrived on the morning of May 19. Unlike his previous devices, Pearce used a rifle bullet, rather than a shotgun cartridge, as ammunition. Luckily, the device did not function when the unsuspecting recipient stripped away the wrapping paper.

On the June 1, another Mardi Gra device — a book, this time wrapped in glossy green paper — arrived at a camera shop in the village of Dymchurch, Kent. The book contained a spring-loaded 7.62mm bullet concealed in its spine. It too failed to detonate.

Eight bombs into his campaign and two bombs into the 'random phase' and Pearce was still finding himself starved of the oxygen of publicity. He wasn't sure if his bombs were getting through to their targets. For him to know that his campaign was working, Pearce had to assure himself that his bombs were getting past the Royal Mail's sorting centres. He decided the best way to find out would be to essentially post a bomb to himself.

This was exactly the moment Roy Ramm and his team had been pushing for. Pearce was being nudged off his plan. In Pearce's dreams this wasn't supposed to happen. In

Pearce's dreams Barclays were meant to pay up as soon as the first demand went in. Now, he was having to ad lib, deviate away from his grand scheme. He obviously recognised the risks. He couldn't just send himself a device — if the police were onto him, it would lead them literally to his door. So he did the next best thing.

The Crown & Anchor pub in Chiswick was Ronald and Edgar's local. Pearce had once even worked there as a cook. However, things had soured there for Pearce, as they had in so many other areas of his life because of his drinking. After an altercation one night as a result of Pearce's rowdy, drunken behaviour, he was barred indefinitely. An extra reason for him to choose the pub as his test target.

Eight days after the Dymchurch bomb, a parcel popped through the front door of the Crown & Anchor. Andy Bennett was the manager of the pub at the time. When the parcel arrived that morning, Andy was about to discover Pearce's unique 'gift' — how an ordinary person enjoying an ordinary day can suddenly find themselves embroiled in something totally beyond their control.

Andy remembers unwrapping the parcel, taking off the brown paper to reveal a black double-sized video case underneath. One of the staff teased him that he was getting blue movies from the post. He smiled and laughed to himself. 'I should be so lucky', he thought and opened the case.

It exploded in his hands. Again, by some miracle of fortune, nobody was seriously hurt.

The night after the attack, Pearce walked into the Crown & Anchor and settled down on a stool at a quiet end of the bar. His ban from the pub long forgotten, he sat, sipping a glass of red wine and waited for the day's gossip to flow around him. He wasn't to be disappointed. The bomb was the only topic of conversation.

Clever Edgar was winning. He celebrated with another drink. And then another.

Now that he knew they were getting through, Pearce dispatched four more bombs over a 23-day period.

The first went back to Barclaycard, just a little reminder that he was still there . . . a rifle bullet, surrounded by gunpowder and lead pellets. The creation was packed inside a plastic bottle. Pearce sent this device deactivated — he left out the firing pin. Whether this was deliberate or a drunken oversight is unclear. Either way, he was demonstrating his potential, showing them what he was capable of, what was coming if they didn't give in to his demands, which this time was for a £10 million payment.

The police quickly tried to make contact with Pearce, placing this advert in the *Daily Telegraph* on June 23:

MARDI GRAS. OK, want to move quickly, but new real problems. Please call me or write.

But Pearce wasn't responding. He wanted to raise the temperature now he knew his bombs were getting through and with a device successfully delivered to the prime target, Pearce went back to random, private addresses, upping the stakes, increasing the pressure.

When selecting whom to attack, Pearce thought carefully about their locations. He wanted them to be far apart because he suspected that the various sorting offices would be looking for his devices. While reassured by the Chiswick pub bomb, he nevertheless reasoned correctly that Post Office staff would be on a heightened state of alert. So he decided to scatter his targets around the south. That way his parcel bombs would have a much better chance of getting through.

He also experimented with various disguises for his bombs — the first of which arrived on the door mat of Dr Christopher Side, a GP from Berkhamstead.

Chris Side has lived and worked in and around the Berkshire towns of Tring and Berkhamstead nearly all his life. He single-handedly runs a small practice of just over 2,000 patients, and, like all doctors has to deal with the unusual, the tragic, the bizarre and the cruel dished out in indiscriminate measure among the community he serves. But on the morning of July 7, it was his turn to be on the receiving end.

At just after 7.00 a.m., as he did every morning, Chris came downstairs to let his dog out into the garden and then went to the front door to collect the day's mail. Among the usual letters and brown enveloped bills was a rolled up copy of the *Radio Times*. Still a bit sleepy, he didn't really wonder what an unsolicited copy of the magazine was doing being posted to his house. Maybe it was a promotion of some sort. Maybe it had just been delivered to the wrong address. Beyond that, as a doctor, he was always receiving journals of one sort or another.

Standing in the hallway, he pulled at the paper seal holding the magazine in its tight roll. As he slit it open . . .

An explosion, like a huge firework going off. Something shot out of the side of the magazine and hit the hallway wall. Upstairs, Chris's wife, Sarah, and their teenage daughter heard the detonation. Downstairs, the doctor was looking at the spot on the wall where whatever had been contained in the magazine had impacted. The magazine tumbled from his grip and landed next to his feet, spilling its contents on to the carpet.

He recalls looking down at what was revealed. 'It was

an interesting device, obviously home made. Part of it was a cylinder which had a spring-loaded arm attached to it. The arm had been held closed by the furled magazine and as it opened, the arm released the spring, which hit the firing pin and the bullet came out the end.

'I didn't really think about it at the time, it was only later when someone asked if it could have damaged me. If I'd been looking into the path of the bullet it would have certainly penetrated my eye.' However, as is his way, he brushes this fact to one side. 'Potentially it was dangerous, but people don't normally open magazines looking down into them.'

Lying alongside the cylinder devices was a poorly photocopied label bearing a poorly typed message — 'With the Compliments of Barclaycard'.

Dr Chris Side, had become part of the Mardi Gra Experience.

The first policeman to attend the scene took one look at the device, which was lying where it fell, and said, 'I think this is the real thing.'

After reporting his finding back to his station, his instructions were unequivocal.

'Get them out, shut the place down'.

After pleading to be allowed to change from their night clothes, the family found themselves being herded from their home, which was then sealed off in preparation for the arrival of the bomb squad.

The rest of the day was to be filled with police and questions. First the local CID and then other detectives, drawn in from the Operation Heath team at Scotland Yard in London. They all asked the same sorts of questions. Had they upset anyone, particularly patients, lately? Had anyone threatened them? Had they ever been involved in animal experimentation? Was there any possible reason they would be an IRA target?

No. No. No. No.

Although, as Chris says, 'The trouble is you can upset people without knowing that you have done it.'

Which was exactly the problem Barclays were facing.

On July 13, a solicitor from Amersham in Buckinghamshire opened a parcel to find a red book, *The Complete Traveller*, inside. As he opened the book, the device hidden inside detonated. Fragments from the explosion hit him next to his right eye. He was lucky to escape with little more than bruising. A fraction more to the side and the debris would have been blasted directly into his eye. Pearce's comments on this device are chilling. 'A book bomb wrapped in children's paper. It needed to look innocuous to defeat the security arrangements.'

On the same day, an inspector for the Inland Revenue living in Surrey found a parcel wrapped in birthday paper on his doorstep. The man called the police and was rewarded for his caution when a Mardi Gra bomb — a twelve-bore shotgun cartridge contained within a cardboard tube, packed with airgun slugs and nails — was found inside, together with the slip which had accompanied all the bombs sent to private addresses: 'With the Compliments of Barclaycard'.

On August 2, another Mardi Gra demand letter was received by Barclaycard.

Until the closing stage of his campaign, and his eventual downfall, Pearce was never one to push his luck. Six bombs into his 'random phase', he decided to change tactics again. This constant switching of targets and bombing methodology was a nightmare for the police. They just didn't know what was coming next.

Despite the fact he was confident his devices were making it through the postal system successfully, Pearce wanted to get even closer to the action, by delivering his bombs personally. It was an interesting decision. On the one hand, he had removed the risk of his devices being intercepted, but on the other he had increased his personal risk in two respects: firstly, the longer he was personally in possession of the device, particularly in public, the greater the chance of being caught. Secondly, there was the physical risk of the bombs going off while he was posting them. The annals of terrorist crime are littered with the body parts of the bomb makers and bomb planters themselves. Bombs by their nature are indiscriminate weapons. They don't care who they blow up, even it that person is their creator.

Pearce was no doubt well aware of this fact and made careful plans to avoid becoming his own victim. For his next five attacks, he chose shops and small businesses. Again, all the targets were random and had no connection either between themselves, to Pearce, or to Barclays. But they did all have one thing in common — low-level letterboxes.

Fearing an accidental discharge, Pearce embarked on a reconnaissance programme to identify targets that suited his purpose and needs. The first of these was slipped through the letterbox of a Kent company based in Welling sometime during the night of August 18. The next day, the parcel was opened and the device — the twelve-bore shotgun cartridge type — activated, but failed to fire.

There then followed the classic Mardi Gra hiatus, lasting almost a month, before he resumed activity, this time with two more attacks on businesses in the same street in the town of Whitton, Middlesex.

On the morning of Tuesday, September 12, Keith Bray had to make sure he was at his electrical business by 8.30am.

As happened every second Tuesday, a rep from one of Keith's suppliers would be coming in to discuss an order. Over the years, the two men had evolved from being customer and salesman to become friends. So it looked like it was going to be a nice gentle start to the day; cup of coffee, a bit of chat, trading gossip on shared acquaintances and bemoaning the highs and lows of the High Street electrical trade.

As he did every day, when Keith arrived at work that morning he went into the shop via the back stairs, in through the back door, turned the lights on and walked through the shop to pick up the post lying behind the front door.

He looked at the stack of envelopes. 'That's a bill, that's a bill, that's a bill,' he muttered to himself. But underneath them was a brown paper parcel about the size of a hardback book. Keith noticed the address label wasn't complete — there was no postcode. He didn't notice, however, that the package had no stamp on it.

'I'd got the best part of the brown paper off and . . . I didn't like it. Call it sixth sense, call it what you like, I didn't like what I was looking at. As I was taking the wrapper off, a little piece of paper dropped out which said "With the Compliments of Barclaycard". It was typed on plain paper with no VISA or Barclaycard logo. So I went and got our contact phone number for them and asked if they were sending out unsolicited parcels.'

The person on the other end of the line at Barclaycard said it wasn't from them, qualifying it with the statement 'we've got a proper compliments slip'. But it's what they didn't do that makes Keith angry.

'I would have thought that the young lady I spoke to, even if she didn't know the full ins and outs of what was going on, should have got enough information from the conversation to think, "I need to transfer this guy to security". But instead all I got was a blank.'

His curiosity roused, Keith went back to his workbench and the package lying half opened on it. Inside that there was corrugated cardboard wrapped around an object.

'I had a look down the side of the tube the cardboard roll formed and saw a shotgun cartridge — and at that point I distinctly heard it go click. I did no more, I rang three nines.'

Because of a bad accident on the A316 that morning, it was more than half an hour before two PCs turned up at the shop. After poking at the parcel with a pen, a call was made back to the station. A sergeant arrived. He took one look at it and ordered the place be evacuated. The bomb squad moved in. A little later Keith got a look at what had been meant for him.

It was a cartridge designed to fire into a glue bottle full of drawing pins.

The device, if it had activated, would have blown pins and lead shot into Keith's face. Essentially, what he had been sent was an anti-personnel nail bomb.

'The anti terrorist guys said it was a proper bomb, but the mechanism it had been made with was not strong enough to activate it. The officers said it might have been a deliberate ploy, that the bomber was sending these just to gain publicity, not really to go off.'

They couldn't have been more wrong. Pearce just hadn't got the technology right. Yet.

While the bomb squad were dealing with the device, a washing machine engineer from R. Jones, another electrical shop further down Whitton High Street, came to Keith's shop to borrow a spare part. Both shops ran in amicable competition swapping the odd part now and again. Rushing back to R. Jones the engineer burst in with the news. 'You'll never guess what's happened? The Bray's have had a bomb down there this morning.' One of the shop girls held up a package she had been shaking next to her ear and said, 'What, was it like this?' The parcel was identical to the one Keith had received. But its passage to its intended victim had not been a direct one. The parcel had originally been delivered to the 'wrong' shop, Kneller Furnishings, located eight doors down from R. Jones. Staff opening up that morning had found the parcel addressed to R. Jones and dropped it back up to them later in the day.

Pearce had carried out reconnaissance on his targets before delivering the bombs, walking up and down the High Street noting which shops had floor-level letter boxes, before deciding on KT Bray and R. Jones as targets. When Pearce returned after the shops closed, he found the Jones' shop protected by a floor to ceiling blue steel shutter which locked the shop windows and door away. No access to the letterbox.

What was he to do? He didn't just want to leave the parcel propped up against the shutters. That would be too suspicious. Or someone else might take off with the parcel. No, he wanted to make sure this shop got it. He carried on walking past more boarded up shops until he found himself outside Kneller Furnishings, with a perfect low letterbox. Stooping over, he carefully pushed the parcel through until he heard the satisfying 'clink' of the metal letterbox cover shut behind the package.

Mission accomplished. Either someone in that shop would open it or, as he gambled correctly, they would take it back up to R. Jones believing the postman had mixed up his delivery.

Pearce's actions that night revealed his determination. He was not going to be stopped, and he wouldn't alter a plan once it was set any more than he absolutely had to. He would not be beaten, not even by a sturdy steel screen. There were always ways round problems. You just had to use a bit of nous.

The bomb had to be delivered, his plan had to be carried out.

He was in control.

After the discovery of the R. Jones device, Keith was taken home by an anti-terrorist officer and interviewed for an hour. The questions would have been familiar to all those targeted by Pearce. Could Keith think of anyone who would do this to him? Did anyone bear a grudge against him? Had he had any problems with customers lately? And again, the answers were all in the negative. There was no connection, there was no-one he knew or had encountered who could have done this.

The rest of the day was a write-off. Keith says, 'I was still very, very shocked. The police had told me not to discuss what had happened with anyone, but I needed to talk. That night, I confided in a friend. He told me to forget it, that I hadn't been targeted personally. But after that conversation, frankly I broke down, I just couldn't hack it. That night I was rough, very rough. I was up most of the night pacing around. I probably drunk the best part of a bottle and a half of scotch.'

Keith's reaction that night is unquestionably the result of delayed shock. How was he to know when he opened that parcel and heard that click that the bomb wasn't live? The fact that it did not explode is almost irrelevant. It is the what might have been, that plays on the mind.

With random violence, victims find themselves desperate to discover 'Why me?' But precisely because it is random there is never an answer.

In Keith's case, he found himself feeling isolated because he couldn't talk about what had happened. And when he finally realised his case was part of the Mardi Gra campaign, he began to get angry at the amount of attention which seemed to be being given to the institutions involved.

'I got very upset when I read about poor Barclays Bank staff, poor Sainsbury's shoppers. What about the eleven of us, the random people? Why were we targeted? Why did no-one report how we felt, how it affected us? No-one knows how many innocent people he affected.'

And now the case is over, what is his opinion of his attacker? 'I want to see him die in prison. I can't see how society can ever afford to let the guy out.'

In the aftermath of the Whitton attacks, the police were still trying to figure out the puzzle. Months were wasted trying to uncover what could possibly link these random incidents, of which there were to be two more directed at businesses — the first on September 27 in Woolwich, the next on October 2 in Chiswick. Both were shotgun devices and both activated when opened. Both contained the bogus Barclaycard compliments slip. No serious injuries, however, resulted.

After the second Chiswick attack, it was obvious to the police that Mardi Gra was back with a vengeance and had settled into a period of sustained activity. Indeed, this 'random phase' of Pearce's was to be the most active of his bombing career. And true to form, while the police were still trying to figure out links between his previous victims, Pearce switched tactics and targets yet again.

Little Box of Horrors

Welcome to the Mardi Gra Experience

One of the factors that most puzzled the public when details of Mardi Gra's campaign were finally revealed to the media, was just how a quiet old man was able to get hold of materials to make bombs that were potentially so lethal they terrified entire communities. Bomb-making has a certain mystique to most people, a mystique drawn from war and spy films. The devices are assumed to be the complex product of much skill. In fact, they are so simple a child could — and has — made them.

Forensics had merely confirmed the profile the police had already drawn up. They were dealing with an amateur, but a good one who was capable of getting much better. For forensic experts working with explosives and firearms, the kind of explosive substance used by an offender is a good rule of thumb indicator of the offender's status. It's a simple delineation. Professionals tend to use high explosives, amateurs low explosives.

Low explosives are chemical mixtures which, when ignited in some way burn at less than the speed of sound — 300 metres per second. Gunpowder is a low explosive. Fireworks are low explosive devices. Firebombs such as those planted by animal rights activists are simple, low-explosive concoctions. Low explosives can also be activated by virtually any method of ignition the bomber chooses, making them incredibly versatile.

A low explosive, though relatively slow burning, generates a phenomenal amount of heat as it combusts. This, in turn, produces gas and, if confined in a small space, can cause huge explosions. In the same way that water always runs to the lowest point, gas always tries to find the easiest route out of its confinement. As soon as it finds the weak point in its container, it bursts through.

High explosives on the other hand, require detonation. Plastic explosives like Semtex or C4 are high explosives, as is dynamite. They can detonate at speeds of up to 9,000 metres per second and the shock waves they generate will shatter anything in their path.

Add to this the refinements practised by organisations like the IRA, such as packing nails and screws around the container containing the explosive, and it's easy to see why their bombs cause so much devastation. A single grain of sand, if caught at the centre of a high explosive detonation, travels with enough velocity to pass straight through a human body. A person hit by a six-inch nail travelling at 9,000 metres per second doesn't stand much chance of survival.

The same principle of packing bombs with nails, razor blades and bits of broken glass can be applied to low-explosive devices and although the resultant shrapnel will be travelling at much lower speeds, its effects can still be devastating. Bombs do not need to be complicated or sophisticated to kill.

Frank Swann is a forensic expert specialising in firearms, munitions, wound ballistics and crime scene reconstructions. He has appeared as an expert witness at every level of the British judicial system from magistrates courts to the Court of Appeal. He is also instructed by the Criminal Cases Review Commission, the independent body charged with examining possible miscarriages of justice. Over the past thirteen years he has cast his expert eye over countless bombing cases and every kind of explosive device has at some time or other passed through his workshop.

Swann offers this interpretation of the differences between professional and 'grudge' bombers:

'A professional bomber is more likely to have access to high explosives and will invariably choose to use these, even though they're difficult to get hold of and the acquisition requires a good support system and a secure line of supply — something beyond the reach of the majority. He will have a cause, usually political, but sometimes can simply be a hired hand, an expert brought in to do a job. Professionals will strike at the 'establishment' and generally try to avoid killing people, although deaths are often inevitable. If they do strike at an individual, it will be someone important or high profile like a judge or a politician. Finally, the bombings of professionals tend to follow a format. Patterns of bombings emerge which clearly identify which group or perpetrators are responsible.

'Amateurs, on the other hand, are unlikely to have any proper training in bomb making and therefore would not have the access to, or the ability to use, high explosives. The attack of an amateur is usually the result of a grudge of some sort and they are much more likely to target individuals rather than institutions.'

The forensic team knew this almost immediately. Technically, the devices weren't really bombs at all, more like glorified fireworks. But it wasn't what they were at this stage that mattered — it was the threat they represented. As time was to tell, these first few devices were mere opening gambits, an indication of what was to come. They were a demonstration of the bomber's power. Only he knew what coming next and where the campaign was going. The ability to keep the police and the country guessing was to be Mardi Gra's greatest weapon.

However, knowing that the Mardi Gra bomber was an amateur using low explosive was of little initial help to the police. And that's the fundamental problem with low explosives. Anyone can make them or get access to them or their constituent parts. Which means any list of people capable of making the Mardi Gra devices would contain tens of millions of names.

This is one of the most disturbing lessons to come from the Mardi Gra case. With a little basic intelligence and technical ability, virtually anyone can get access to the knowledge to make lethal explosive devices. Just how easy is it? As easy as reading a book or logging onto the internet.

Using a common Internet search engine, type in the phrase 'bomb making' and you'll get more than 2,000 hits. Among the legitimate news stories and discussion papers called up, you'll come across a frightening number of do-it-yourself bomb sites.

Refine the search slightly, and you'll find sites which offer not only explicit bomb-making instructions, but in some cases advice on how to select targets and locations to cause maximum injury. There are schematic diagrams for improvised land mines, time bombs, grenades and fire bombs; circuit diagrams for electronic timers; chemical recipes for explosive mixtures. On one page there's even a recipe for home-made napalm.

It would be easy to dismiss these sites as being just the work of fringe extremists or reckless individuals hiding behind the excuse that they are 'anarchists'. But the availability of bomb-making know-how isn't restricted to these odd sites anchored out in cyberspace. You can get hard copies too.

With a few clicks of the mouse, the Internet shopper can have access to literally dozens of bomb-making books. Stopping off at one site I am offered a book by an author called Seymour Lecker who, according to the publicity blurb, is a 'former top explosives expert with the Israeli Army'. In his 'all new manual' the reader is offered, 'ten simple formulas for constructing bombs, booby traps and mines. How to obtain or make all the necessary chemicals or acceptable substitutes. Various fuses, detonators and electrical timers are covered, as are pipe bombs, plastic bottle bombs, jerry can bombs and tamperproof bombs.'

The blurb proudly concludes, 'You can construct such devices as a package bomb, booby-trapped door, auto trap, sound-detonated bomb or pressure mine, to name just a few.'

And all for just $11.95. A bargain to set the world on fire . . .

However, being offered such knowledge and actually getting your hands on it are two different things. Or are they? In America, the authorities cannot control the dissemination of such material, which finds protection under the First Amendment guaranteeing freedom of speech. But, it could be argued that in Britain, given our bitter experience of terrorism and our attempts to contain and control it, there would be safeguards to ensure these sort of books don't reach these shores. Sadly, that is not the case at all.

At another on-line book seller Mr Lecker has eight other books published, all on the same themes — 'Improvised Explosives — How To Make Your Own', 'Home-made Semtex' and 'Poor Man's TNT' to name a few. And if you want to go in depth there's 'Guerrilla's Arsenal — Advanced Techniques for Making Explosives and Time-Delay Bombs'.

The book's jacket proclaims that this work is 'a complete primer on the art and science of making explosives from scratch using them in one of the most potent weapons in the unconventional warfare specialist's arsenal — the time bomb'. This sets the tone of the book, which rapidly reveals its genesis; a backwoods paranoia peculiar to America.

'This book may seem controversial and dangerous,' the jacket's introduction continues, 'but such information may someday be the lifeblood of freedom fighters under the oppressive thumb of a tyrannical government that has secured all means of force unto itself.'

Then: 'The procedures described herein are presented for information purposes only.'

Of course they are.

It's all too easy to dismiss the danger this sort of book represents. Surely only war games wannabes and masturbatory teenage boys are going to want to read this stuff and out of them, how many are actually going to be stupid enough to risk their lives trying to actually put the theory into practice?

Welcome to the Mardi Gra Experience

Dismiss this: three days after Edgar Pearce was sentenced at the Old Bailey, Brixton market in London was ripped apart by a nail bomb planted, it is believed, by neo-Nazi racists. It was a simple, low-explosive time bomb packed with between six to eight pounds of nails. Fifteen people were hurt, including a 23-month-old boy, who had a six-inch nail embedded in his brain as a result of the blast. Miraculously, the boy escaped death and was successfully operated on to remove the nail.

Three days after the Brixton blast, two teenage boys walked into their school in Littleton, Colorado. Armed to the teeth with guns and home-made explosives, teenagers Eric Harris and Dylan Klebold proceeded to kill thirteen fellow pupils and teachers and wound dozens more.

At around 11.00 a.m. on Tuesday April 20, 1999, Harris and Klebold began their attack by hurling pipe bombs outside the school. They booby trapped cars with the bombs and as they made their way through the school shooting, they augmented their assault with more pipe bombs. At 11.35 cars began to explode, while inside there were explosions in the school's cafeteria and snack room. That day, there were fifteen explosions in all. The SWAT teams which eventually cleared the school, found a total of 30 devices, one of which was wired to a massive gas tank, the intention being to blow the entire school, and everyone in it, sky high. Throughout the building, the killers had broken off the gas taps in the science labs, hoping the gas which haemorrhaged from the exposed pipes would increase the blast.

The pipe bombs used by Harris and Klebold are a staple favourite of apocalyptic U.S. militias and teenage pyromaniacs. Indeed, it was a pipe bomb, packed with nails, which exploded during the 1996 Atlanta Olympics, killing one person and injuring around a hundred others.

More than a third of all bomb incidents dealt with by American law enforcement officials are the work of teenagers with home-made devices of this nature. The 'Guerrilla's Arsenal' devotes a whole chapter to them, informing the reader that 'a properly made and employed pipe bomb can be very destructive when utilised against both personnel and material in an unconventional warfare setting'.

An unconventional warfare setting. That must mean the slaughter of twelve children and a teacher.

Four days after the Colorado massacre, another nail bomb erupted in London, this time in the East End's Brick Lane, the former heartland of the city's vibrant Jewish community and now the Bangladeshi centre of the capital. Again, neo-Nazi racists were thought to be responsible.

Friday April 30: a nail bomb left in the Admiral Nelson pub in London's Soho detonated. In the enclosed environment of the pub, the blast claimed the lives of three people and seriously injured more than 70 others. Those who survived had limbs torn off, suffered terrible burns and were left with six-inch nails, glass and fragments of metal embedded in their bodies. Professor Gus McGrouther, the plastic surgeon who treated many of the survivors, said, 'these injuries are as bad, if not worse, than many of those inflicted among war victims. They're not going to get better in a week or two. They are going to be mutilated for life.'

If ever an incident demonstrated the indiscriminate nature of the bomb as a weapon of terror, it was this one. The target of the device was the gay community, which centres around Soho. Among the fatalities was Andrea Dykes, who was three months pregnant when she died.

What the Mardi Gra bomber, the Colorado killers and

the London nail-bombings reveal is a truth which police find extremely uncomfortable and are understandably loathe to admit or discuss. With the amateur bomber, you will never know what is intended or what his capabilities are until the bomb has gone off.

Prevention is impossible. And there may be no cure.

Bombs can be hidden in anything — portable radios (Pan Am, Lockerbie), cassette boxes (the IRA's Oxford Street campaign), cigarette packets (animal rights activists), books. Pearce used video cases, magazines, bin bags, shopping bags and books.

Any housing will do.

Swann has a whole collection of samples. A pack of Embassy cigarettes on the outside. Inside a condom filled with acid. Around the condom is packed sugar and an accelerant. The acid eats through the latex of the condom and reacts with the explosive mixture, generating enough heat to start a fire. It's a crude device, because there's no way of controlling the rate of acid eating through the latex and there is therefore a danger it will ignite in the pocket or hands of the person planting it.

Next up is a small parcel, triggered by a simple light-reactive diode. 'The minute you open the box and light falls on it — boom! That's it,' says Swann. It's the kind of device the IRA used to send to Army officers and the RUC.

Then there's the type of device Pearce preferred — a variation on the classic 'book bomb'. The pages of a hardback are cut out and replaced with explosives, detonated by the release of a spring held in place by the book's cover. 'It's very basic, quite simple, in fact so simple it's brilliant really.' comments Swann. 'You can make the components yourself or you can buy them complete; the spring detonators are readily available from sporting shops and have a definitive sporting use for all sorts of things — bird scarers, anti-poacher devices, but they are so easy to alter to suit your own purpose.' Pearce, with his instinctive knowledge of machines and electronics, had no problem in customising them suit his purposes, often spending up to three days constructing each devices from these basic parts. 'Your DIY bomber just needs a bird scarer, a hooky supply of cartridges and he's away,' confirms Swann.

This was exactly how Pearce started, using video cases as his containers. Shotgun cartridges, bought in France and smuggled back in the fifty-odd boxes of wine he would buy at a time, were loaded in front of a compressed spring, which powered the firing pin when the video case was opened.

And it's capabilities? 'If you had it in your hand and it went off it's just like a grenade. All the pellets come out and go everywhere. The person holding the device would be smothered in ball bearings. Without a barrel to direct the shot, the victim would be hit by about 25% of the material, but at very close range, the explosion along with the pellets could prove fatal.'

Factor in the added extras Pearce included in later incarnations of his basic shotgun cartridge bomb, such as placing containers of drawing pins in front of the cartridge, and you have a lethal threat.

All these devices are easy to manufacture with little equipment and it can be done under the noses of most people without them ever realising what is going on. After the Colorado massacre conducted by Eric Harris and Dylan Klebold, one distraught parent raged, 'How out of touch are you with your kid that you don't know he's making 30 bombs?'

The answer is a chilling one. You don't have to be out of touch at all. Bombs can be made anywhere presenting police with an unsolvable problem. It's usually only after someone is publicly accused of a serious crime that the people around them are able to put together all the little things they may have noticed about their behaviour. 'I knew there was something going on,' they say, 'I should have seen it, I should have noticed something was wrong.' Hindsight. Everyone's an expert after the fact.

In Denver, one neighbour of Eric Harris recalled how on the day before the massacre he heard the boys smashing up the glass behind the closed door of a garage. The boys packed their bombs with the shards. 'He was always in there with the door closed,' said a teenager who lived in the area. And anyone logging onto Harris' Internet web page would have found he had written instructions on bomb construction, telling his viewers that the pipe bomb is the 'easiest and deadliest way' of killing people and more sinisterly proclaiming, 'I will rig up explosives all over town. I don't care if I live or die.'

The point is, unless you're looking for it, nine times out of ten it's just not obvious. Take the example of Sue Hinchcliffe, who for a short while lodged in one of Edgar Pearce's rooms. One morning, Sue wandered into the communal kitchen to make a cup of tea and found Pearce beavering away at the kitchen table. A soldering iron smoking in one hand, a circuit board in the other, Pearce seemed totally absorbed in his work. Scattered across the table were other bits of wire, metal and plastic. She asked him what he was up to and he replied, 'Nothing. Just a little hobby of mine.' He then calmly packed up his 'hobby' into a plastic carrier bag and wandered off down to the greenhouse at the foot of the overgrown garden. Sue thought nothing of it until the story broke.

Are we suspicious yet? The next time you see a neighbour messing around with a length of pipe and fireworks, will you call the police? Of course you won't. Unless people feel directly threatened they tend to do nothing. And more importantly, there is a reservoir of reserve centred on our unwillingness to look foolish if our suspicions turn out to be unfounded. No matter how many times the police say they would rather be called out to a false alert than have people ignore a suspicious package, the Good Samaritan story still holds true — most pass by on the other side.

The lone bomber. Indiscriminate. Unpredictable. Unknown.

Invisible.

How do you catch the invisible man?

Every Detective's Nightmare

Welcome to the Mardi Gra Experience

Pearce was predictably unpredictable. The very randomness of his attacks had a pattern to them. It became his trademark as much as his snappy logo and neat imagery. Pearce kept switching tactics and targets to keep the police guessing. 'The more I move about', he thought, 'the more time they'll waste tracking down trails which have already come to a dead end.' He would also tinker with the design of his devices creating a whole host of variations on his basic shotgun cartridge model. Again, he knew every variation would force the police down new lines of inquiry. Let them play with theories. Only one man knew the reality. And he intended to keep it that way for as long as possible.

Pearce had delivered his latest device at the beginning of October and in the weeks that followed he roamed around west London looking for another target. Despite their separation, Pearce and Maureen remained on good terms and would see each other regularly. Maureen would come to Cambridge Road North one week, Pearce would go to her flat in Welling the next. It is now known Pearce did a lot of his reconnaissance while on his visits to Maureen — and indeed planted devices in and around the area in which she lived.

On October 24, Pearce left another bomb, this time inside a telephone box in Welling. It was made out of a long tube with a spring-loaded metal arm lying flat against the outside of the tube, restrained by the brown paper it was wrapped in. The package bore the message 'Another smashing free gift from Barclays' — a clear incitement to the curious to open it. Like the devices sent to Dr Chris Side and Keith Bray, this bomb was designed to fire when the tension on the arm was released by the removal of the paper. The device was armed with Pearce's explosive of choice — a shotgun cartridge fired by a nail. It is not known how long the bomb lay there after Pearce had lumbered away, but when it was found it was taken immediately to the local police station.

Three more phone box bombs followed. At the beginning of his campaign, Pearce had tinkered in his room, or in the kitchen, but soon the sheer frequency and intricacy of the devices he was making meant he had to spread out. There was ample space in the secluded, overgrown greenhouse halfway down his garden. He had the greenhouse converted into his workshop, and for power supply trailed an extension cable out through the back kitchen window and along fifteen feet of fence and trellising. Inside he placed a couple of small aluminium framed chairs and rigged up some waist-high shelving, which doubled as a work surface. He would potter to and from the house to the greenhouse with carrier bags full of bits and pieces. Looking from the house, the greenhouse was completely shielded from view by the climbers and shrubs which had, over the years crept over and around it. Now, Pearce could work in total privacy, late into the night if need be, a bare light bulb burning above his balding head. This odd behaviour was dismissed by his lodgers as just another example of their landlord's eccentricity. Their landlord, the midnight gardener. 'I just thought he had some herbs or something in there,' said one tenant later.

The next device was found on November 20 by two sixteen-year-olds on Eltham High Road. Pearce reverted to his original type of shotgun bomb to ensure an explosion that would get the message across to the police that he meant business. However, things didn't go to plan. Yet again, it failed to go off.

Southall and Acton phone box bombs followed in December. All bore the inviting strapline, 'Another smashing free gift from Barclays'.

One year and twenty-one bombs later, police had made absolutely no progress. Mardi Gra obstinately refused to engage in dialogue, despite having sent three demand letters. The tone of the letters was worrying for detectives. Pearce was upping the ante by threatening ever more violent reprisals unless his demands were met. 'Now we are talking serious grenade business,' he wrote ominously in one. The police's frustration and concern is transparently clear in one message they posted for Pearce in the *Daily Telegraph* earlier in 1995.

MARDI GRAS. Why keep doing this if you will not talk? Your request is impossible, but I still want to help you somehow. It is very important you call me urgently on [telephone number withheld] We must end this stalemate now. We can then carry on with our lives.

Back in Specialist Operations at the Met, Commander Roy Ramm was considering the possibility that they were dealing with someone totally deranged. 'I have to admit we wondered if he was all there. What was his plan? What if he didn't really have one, and was just doing this for fun.' That was the nightmare scenario — a bomber who really didn't care if his demands were met, because he was enjoying the game too much. If that were the case the stakes would only increase, because as everyone knows, if you keep playing the same game over and over, it gets boring. You need to keep changing the rules to add a little spice.

The hunt for the Mardi Gra bomber was, to quote former Greater Manchester deputy chief constable John Stalker, 'A detective's nightmare.' In a one-page article for the Sun analysing the bomber and his campaign, he encapsulated perfectly the enormity and the impossibility of the task facing the Met. 'Mardi Gra is,' he said, 'a grey face operating intermittently in a city of seven million people.'

How do you hunt the invisible man? From an investigator's point of view, this case was continually frustrating. Once the Barclays lists had been exhausted there was nothing else to go on. No forensics, no eye witnesses, no video recordings, no leads from the sale of materials, nothing. Not even the odd dead end to wander up with a bit of hope. The police didn't know who Mardi Gra was, what he looked like, where he was from, or why he was doing this.

They didn't know, because Pearce was expert at covering his tracks. He knew materials used in bombs could usually be traced back to the point of sale, so to combat this he only bought his components from non-traceable sources — usually car boot sales. He always paid for everything in cash to make sure there was no paper trail, including in France when he bought his ammunition. During the bomb-manufacturing process, he went to extraordinary lengths to avoid leaving fingerprints or any other evidence. He filed the edges of the wooden boards he mounted the devices on into smooth round surfaces — the police originally thought this was an indication of an older man taking pride in his work. In fact, Pearce told police he sanded the edges to make sure he didn't cut himself on any splinters and leave blood which could be used for DNA evidence. All the devices were washed with petrol and sprayed black once completed, a last failsafe for Pearce just in case he had made a mistake and left a fingerprint. The only thing forensic scientists found at any time during the investigation were some tiny blue fibres on a couple of the devices, but they were to be of no help as they came from the gloves Pearce wore when making the bombs. The brand was a common one, bought by millions around the country.

Pearce was also very surveillance conscious and had managed by luck or design to dodge both town-centre CCTV cameras and the security cameras used by his victims. This lack of any image of the bomber meant it wasn't until Pearce's very last attack on March 17, 1998, that the police really knew for the first time they were dealing with a lone bomber rather than a criminal gang.

The possibility that the bombs were the work of a gang had been considered from the very earliest days of the investigation. When Pearce decided to take his campaign public, he wrote to two newspapers purporting to represent an activist organisation. In a letter sent to the *Daily Mail* on April 3, 1996, Pearce said he was representing a group of disaffected Barclays customers.

In theory, having a group of people to investigate would have made the police's job easier simply because the more people are involved in a crime, the more chance there is that one of them will be on a database somewhere or will make a mistake, or will talk. But well-organised criminal and terrorist gangs have spotted this chink in their armour and devised new methods of organisation and operation. David Capitanchik, a terrorism expert at Aberdeen University, says, 'A group is easy to infiltrate once it has grown to the extent that people don't all know each other. But the very small groups work on the theory that if you have a tiny cell, there's much less chance of them being caught, and, if they are busted, it is only that cell that suffers, not the organisation it works for.'

As far as we know, Pearce was working alone until close to the very end of his campaign. (Although, Edgar's brother Ronald was also charged, there was no proof that Edgar had involved his brother from the beginning, or even that Ronald was aware of what was going on.) The investigators running Operation Heath were almost sure they were dealing with a loner but they had to keep every possibility open to further enquiries. For the reasons stated above, some members of the team wished it were a criminal gang — at least then they would know what they were dealing with.

In an article which ran just after Mardi Gra's campaign was finally made public by the police, the *Daily Mirror* quoted an unnamed SO13 officer who offered a frank admission as to the difficulties they were facing — and hinted at dire consequences of staying in the dark. 'We can't even be sure if we're looking for a man or a woman. Although this person started off with a complex plan to steal very large sums of money, it may be that he has other things on his mind. There are a host of reasons why someone may have it in for a bank and want to extract some sort of retribution.

'We just don't know what's motivating this person. It might be game-playing . . . It's a very bizarre affair. Whoever's involved is very clever, but must be unhinged and it's imperative that we get to the bottom of the case quickly.'

Which, as their experience with Mardi Gra to date had shown, was much easier said than done. 'The difficulty with kidnap and blackmail is their infrequency,' explains ex-Commander Ramm. 'I used to lecture on blackmail at Bramshill Police Training College. I'd say to the investigators, even if you weren't police officers I could take you to a station like Paddington or Stoke Newington in London and teach you how to be a burglary investigator in a month. You wouldn't be the greatest in the world, but you'd get by because every day there'd be five or six cases coming in.

'To become a good extortion investigator, however, I'd have to shove someone in a van and take them around the country to each individual police station which had dealt with a blackmail case. Acquiring the body of knowledge is very difficult. The second problem is that if I make you a burglary investigator and I take you along and you mess it up, the worst thing you can do is not catch the person who did it. You're not likely to make matters worse. With a blackmail, you actually have a crime in progress. The thing is going on while it is being investigated and if you do something wrong you have the unique opportunity of being able to precipitate either the threatened offence or something far worse.'

The other great obstacle facing the blackmail investigator is a practical one. Blackmail and extortion are crimes that are boundary free. No matter where the blackmailer bases himself, his targets can be anywhere in the country, and the threats themselves are made wherever the blackmailer desires — to newspapers, individual branches of the target company or to local police stations. The blackmailer has the ability to involve several police forces in his crimes, adding another level of logistical and administrative difficulty for the lead investigating officers.

The effect of a drawn-out campaign of extortion on an investigation team also brings its own unique problems. Roy Ramm, faced with an enquiry which potentially could run for years, could not afford to lighten the inevitable fatigue which set in as the weeks and months dragged by. 'The problem is that the blackmailer fixes the timetable. If I was running a one-off murder investigation and I had been working my team really hard and I could see they were getting weary I can say, "OK guys, you're not going to bring the victim back, so unless there's a really pressing line of enquiry let's stop at four. Enjoy your weekend, come back fresh first thing Monday." You can't do that with blackmail, or if you do, there's no guarantee the team are going to get the break they need. The extortionist could drop one on you any time day or night. He's pulling the strings, he's driving the location and the time scale.'

Which makes this sort of investigation a war of psychological and sometimes, physical attrition. It is conducted as much in the minds of those involved as it is on the streets. With no real evidential trail to follow and no likely faces to pull in for questioning, investigators have to get into the head of the blackmailer. Unless the blackmailer comes out to show himself, the odds are he will never be caught. The trick is to lure him out.

When a blackmail investigation starts, the first job for the investigating team is to make a thorough risk assessment. How dangerous is this person? What's the risk to the public? Can the threats being made to the company be realistically carried out? 'You have to set the parameters,' says Ramm. 'You know that whatever you do you cannot afford to substantially increase the risk of people being killed or injured.'

John O'Connor is the former commander of the Met's famous Flying Squad. An officer of more than twenty years' service, he dealt with numerous serious blackmail attempts. The investigator's approach, he says, begins with the target. 'First you have to look at what they are threatening to attack. If it's a product, say baked beans, what's the security on that product, what's the security on the packaging? It comes down to what is the likelihood that the person is going to be able to actually carry out their threats. How's he going to poison the baked bean tins? If he's capable, then it's probably an employee, so extra security can be mounted around the production area. If you think the beans are going to be adulterated once they've got to the supermarket shelf, then you stick extra security on those sections of the supermarket. A visible security presence is a very good deterrent.'

However, when the demand first comes in a company will usually try to handle the situation itself. 'Often it won't even get to the police,' says O'Connor. 'Experienced guys in corporate security will assume it's some crank or a hoax — and only respond when it's too late. If Pearce hadn't bombed first, his demand would have been ignored.'

It may seem to the reader that this is a callous disregard for public safety but the problem is that threats come in one way or another almost every week. Indeed, the most experienced security experts have difficulty sifting the real threats from the imagined. Even when it gets specific, for example a letter demanding a message in the personal columns (as O'Connor puts it, 'it's always some crap like "Romeo wants to play. Juliet" ') the threats are all too common to act upon every time. In the past companies would always respond, but then blackmail was a rare occurrence. In recent years, the frequency of this approach to 'customer complaints' has escalated to the extent that businesses simply don't have the time or resources to deal with them effectively. That's not to say that they are ignored altogether. These days letters are graded, because the minute a company responds to a threat of this nature, they are upping the ante. By taking note but not responding, a company can stay aware of the potential problem (maybe heightening security in their stores) whilst avoiding encouraging a crank/extortionist further. Once someone thinks they've got a reaction, they might take it further. If a would-be blackmailer thinks they've got a company frightened they might actually take it further. 99 times out of 100 if they're ignored, they'll go away. Because it's easy to write nasty letters but it's a big leap to plant a bomb. That, of course, still leaves the one in a hundred that might slip through the net . . .

Mike Bluestone, who runs the Berkley Security Bureau, a corporate security consultancy, expands on this theme. 'There are a lot more incidents than reach the public eye — for obvious reasons. No High Street name is going to want the public to know that they've been the victim of even an attempted blackmail because it can ruin their image and their profits. So a lot will try and be sorted quietly. Having said that, there is extremely close co-operation between heads of security and the police. A company's accountability to its customers is always at the forefront of decision making, but it's a judgement call based on the circumstances and on the threat assessment.'

That companies play a potentially deadly game of show and tell with dozens of blackmailers every year is worrying. In doing so they tread a fine line. Weighing the theoretical possibility of attack against the risk that a customer may end up choking on a sliver of razor blade or being blown up leaves a company extremely vulnerable to accusations of putting profit before people. Companies defend themselves against this by pointing out that most threats come to nothing; the first letter is usually the last.

Once the threat is made real, the investigators must try and figure out what the motive is. Surprisingly, the primary motive is usually revenge, not greed — a disgruntled former employee or a 'wronged' customer who wants to play David against Goliath. With the

Mardi Gra bomber it wasn't clear what category he came into — whether it was someone hell bent on causing havoc or whether it was a commercial criminal enterprise.

From the moment Pearce's first demand was received by Barclays on December 8, 1994, police and the company's security team had been combing back through personnel and customer files looking for anyone who might have the motivation to embark on violent revenge. They were looking for something, no matter how small, that might be the grain of information which lead to the resolution of the case.

'On every major enquiry I ever ran, I never rubbished anyone, never discouraged anybody from the lowest cadet, PC, whatever, from coming forward with a name,' says O' Connor. 'I didn't care how big the database was, because the bigger the database the more likely it was that the suspect was in there. I just wanted the information, even if the reason behind it being offered was malicious or even if the information being given was totally false and misleading. Because once it's in the system, you can get it out again. Look at what the Mardi Gra team had — no evidence, no idea who's done it, but what they did have was their database of suspects. So you work through it, trying to prioritise the most likely and then you go through it and you eliminate them. But if that suspect isn't in the database, it doesn't matter how long you work it. You ain't going to find anything if it's not in there.'

The suspect list from Barclays was 2,000 strong. Pearce's name wasn't on it.

While the monotonous paper chase continued, Ramm and his team were embarking on the most dangerous aspect of any blackmail investigation — trying to draw the blackmailer out. Ramm calls this process 'fly fishing'. This technique usually works, because as O'Connor explains, 'Blackmailers act on the urban myth that companies pay out all the time. Guys like Pearce firmly believe that companies will play lap dog to make guys like him go away. Nothing could be further from the truth.'

For the blackmailer, the riskiest part of the crime is collecting the money. As soon as a blackmailer sets out to collect, they're vulnerable and present the police with their best — and possibly only — chance to make an arrest. Ramm's 'fly fishing' is designed to tempt the blackmailer quickly into this stage of his plan . 'We give them the impression that all we want them to do is go away, that if paying them is what it takes, then we'll do it. Then as soon as they are drawn into a dialogue, we start to prevaricate.'

This prevarication is designed to push the blackmailer further off the path of his plan. The police will respond eagerly to start with, making contact exactly as the blackmailer has stipulated. But as soon as the police get a bite, they will start to back off, building delays into the negotiations by telling the blackmailer there are problems or that the demand is not possible in one form, but may be possible in another. If the blackmailer is determined to get to the money, he will engage in a dialogue about this and once engaged, he is effectively in open water and away from his planned course.

And once he's in open water, the police control the current and it becomes a battle to see if the blackmailer sinks or swims.

Running alongside the negotiation strategy Ramm's team had decided upon, the straightforward criminal investigation continued. But the officers found themselves hobbled by the earlier decision to enforce a news blackout. Included in this blackout were Barclays own staff (as Kevin Bray found out to his anger). It was a decision which later brought furious condemnation from the banking unions, who accused Barclays of deliberately putting its staff and customers at unnecessary risk for the sake of profit. In fairness, the blackout was a tactical decision made in conjunction with the police and a warning, albeit vaguely worded, was placed on cashpoint screens asking people to be aware of suspicious packages.

Ramm remembers the blackout bringing 'another whole raft of problems' for the team. 'The first phrase you learn at police training school is, "Did anyone see what happened?" Now with blackmail you have to think, if I go knocking on 100 doors asking about this incident, what's that going to do to my covert investigation? Do I think there's going to be any evidence out there, what's the value of that evidence weighed against disclosing the investigation. It's a tough call because keeping quiet goes against the grain. We might lose a witness by not knocking on all those doors.'

The secrecy effectively robbed the police of one of its best intelligence gathering conduits — the eyes and ears of the public. This lack of feedback cut them off from Mardi Gra's street level operation. After all, if no one knows to keep an eye out, they're not going to see anything. This lack of feedback made it all the more urgent that the police get some breakthrough that would bring them closer to the bomber.

That urgency increased as 1995 became 1996. Mardi

Gra was still at large.

On January 30, 1996 a briefcase left on the pavement near a Barclays branch in South Ealing Road erupted in flames. The ball of fire shot out into the road, engulfing a passing car. 999 calls soon began to flood in and the area was sealed off. In the debris left on the pavement the bomb squad found the remains of a helium gas cylinder. This was odd as helium is non-flammable and therefore could not have been responsible for the explosion. Sure enough, when the cylinder was examined by forensic scientists they discovered the gas bottle had been emptied and refilled with a petrol-based gas.

Delighted with the explosive success of this latest bomb, Pearce decided to go back to attacking Barclays directly. Fourteen months in, he was getting nowhere, although as it later emerged, he had prepared himself for a long campaign, a campaign he felt confident to wage from within the safety of his anonymity. Barclays itself had had it easy recently. If they wouldn't tell the public what was happening he'd turn the heat up until they had to . . .

He quickly followed his January 30 strike — which occurred less than a mile from his own front door — with another attack on a Barclays branch in Eltham.

A council dustman working his way down the High Street grabbed a handful of the rubbish bags stacked up outside the bank for collection. As he went to move away he caught a whiff of an unmistakable smell. Gas. He sniffed the air a few times. It seemed strongest by the rubbish bags. In fact it coming from one of the bags, a green one. The dustman took a peek inside the bag and there sat a small blue Calor gas cylinder. Attached to its side was a white plastic box with wires running to the neck of the cylinder. The dustman immediately called the police and did his best to clear the area. The explosives officers arriving on the scene swiftly deactivated the device and again, by a miracle no-one was hurt by a Pearce device. But this latest bomb revealed to detectives the extraordinary lengths Mardi Gra was prepared to go to in order to make his point.

'Do not ignore me,' he was saying. 'And don't you dare mess with me. If you do, you'll be sorry.'

When police searched 12 Cambridge Road North, they found six similar devices being prepared. Each cylinder was twinned with a gas igniter which Pearce was in the process of modifying by adding an electronic timer. Pearce later told police he started experimenting with them after hearing on the news that the IRA used them. The gas cylinder bombs Pearce had begun to experiment with are horrific in their potential. If it had gone off, anybody within 50-60 yards would have been badly hurt from fire and shrapnel injuries. Close by and it would have been almost certain death.

Pearce had no idea if his gas bombs would work. He simply left them in the street in the hope that they would. In a police interview he revealed his total inability to comprehend the real danger of what he was doing or the possible consequences. 'It would have been dangerous in a confined space. In an open space it would not have been . . . There were two of these, one in Eltham, one in Ealing. Both were open spaces. I didn't think either were particularly manageable.'

Asked specifically about January 30 attack, where Scott Anderson received burns to his face, Pearce replies flatly, 'I hadn't tested that type. This was a field test. I thought it would burst into flames, not explode.'

The advent of the gas bombs hardened the police's opinion that they were living on borrowed time, that one day one of Mardi Gra's bombs was going to cause a fatality. That day seemed to be getting ever closer if the new devices were anything to go by.

No-one wanted to contemplate what was coming next.

The Perfect Blackmailer

Welcome to the Mardi Gra Experience

Whoever thinks a faultless piece to see
Thinks what ne'er was, nor is, nor shall be

Alexander Pope, *An Essay on Criticism*

For the Met in particular, the crime of blackmail is a nightmare not only because of the difficulties it presents to investigating detectives. It's a nightmare because it brings back bad memories. . .

The greatest betrayal the Met ever experienced was revealed during one of the most complex police investigations of all time, an investigation set up in response to an aggressive blackmail campaign mounted in the late 1980s. The conclusion of that enquiry and the unmasking of the blackmailer sent a shudder through the entire British police service.

It was the Met's darkest hour. Their investigation revealed the force had been infiltrated by the blackmailer himself.

The case concerned the infamous 'Baby Food Blackmailer.'

The blackmailer was a man called Rodney Whitchelo.

Is there such a thing as the perfect crime? Rodney Whitchelo thought so and he had good reason to be confident. As a detective sergeant in a branch of one of Britain's elite Regional Crime Squads, he knew the way criminals were caught, the mistakes they made and the secret techniques employed by the police to trap them. The perfect crime, reasoned Whitchelo, would have to be an unsolvable one, the perfect criminal untraceable. Was this possible? Of course it was — if the policeman hunting the perfect criminal was the criminal himself. And what about the crime? Whitchelo knew the answer to that too — blackmail. With his police career stalled and his ambitions thwarted, Whitchelo decided it was time to put his unrewarded talents to use.

Like most extortions, it started with an innocuous-looking item of mail. MD of Pedigree Pet Foods, John Simmens opened his to find inside:

This is a demand to Pedigree Pet Foods to pay £100,000 a year in order to prevent its products being contaminated with toxic substances. The accompanying tin of Pedigree Pet food has had the contents mixed with biocides. These chemicals were selected because they are colourless, odourless and highly toxic.

They are virtually undetectable by a pet owner before feeding the contaminated product to their dog. If payment is not forthcoming from Pedigree Pet Foods or Mars Limited, a large number of similarly contaminated tins will appear on retailers' shelves.

The letter's author was Rodney Whitchelo and it was the product of almost two years plotting and preparation by the man who was to about to enter criminal history as one of the most corrupt policemen ever to serve in a British force. His extortion letter, received in August 1988 at Pedigree Pet Food's company headquarters went on to describe in detail his demands, the way the company should respond to them and what would happen if they didn't.

To facilitate public awareness the media will anonymously be notified daily of five locations where such tins have been placed. The code words Romeo and Juliet will be quoted on each occasion.

If payment is not made, the threat will be carried out progressively. Initially, only Pedigree Chum dog food will be poisoned. When sales of that product have slumped, another will be sabotaged if payment has not yet been received, for example Pal, Whiskas, Mr Dog etc.

The process will be repeated until payment is finally made or your company dissolved. Its fate will then be an example for other pet food manufacturers, such as Spillers. When your company agrees to pay it will place an announcement in the personal column of the Daily Telegraph which will read, 'Sandra, happy birthday darling, love John.'

The sum of £100,000 will be demanded annually for five years after which no further demands will be made.

Analysis of the accompanying tin of dog food did indeed reveal contamination. The label had been lifted and the tin perforated by a tiny drilled hole. Poison had been injected and the tin then resealed, with the label glued back down to hide the hole. If the threat was real and followed through, the consequences for the company would be dire. At a conference between police and the company's senior management, a plan was agreed. Money would be paid over as demanded. They then had to pray that when the blackmailer moved to collect the cash, he would reveal himself.

Rodney Whitchelo had been a late starter as far as his police career was concerned. A bright student with good 'O' levels behind him, he quit his 'A' level courses half-way through to go straight into the world of work. He joined Plessey in 1967 where he graduated top of his course in electronic engineering, but nine years later, at the age of 29, Whitchelo decided this career did not suit him. He wanted, he said, 'To do something that involved people.' That something, he concluded, was the police. He duly signed up and in 1976 came top of his class at Hendon police training college. If he was an impressive recruit, he went on to be an even more impressive serving officer, moving smoothly up through the ranks. He trained and qualified as a firearms officer, passed the detectives' course and his sergeants' exam.

For a while Whitchelo found life fulfilling. While based at Gerald Road police station, he was part of the team involved in investigating how Michael Fagin was able to break into Buckingham Palace during the night and make his way into the Queen's bedroom, where he sat on her bed and chatted with a startled Her Majesty until being hauled away by Royal Protection officers. This incident was to later provide fuel for a 'Walter Mitty' fantasy complex which Whitchelo was beginning to develop. He was to tell friends that he had taken the Queen's statement following the break in. 'I found it difficult to keep a straight face,' he claimed. 'The Queen was rather cross, particularly when a policeman came sauntering along the corridor and went into the wrong room. She said, "I was quite exasperated. If the Duke of Edinburgh had been here, it would have been a different story."' The entire encounter was nothing more than a product of Whitchelo's weird imagination. As he was to progress from policeman to criminal he was to invent other, similar fantastic tales. He had infiltrated the IRA; he had been held at gunpoint; he was a millionaire computer tycoon. He was whatever he wanted to be.

Fantasies aside, Whitchelo continued to enjoy success in the force, becoming a detective sergeant with Number 9 Regional Crime Squad, Barkingside, east London. But the upwards curve was beginning to flatten out. In 1986, as Whitchelo approached his fortieth birthday, he came to the conclusion that his time in the force was nearing an end. Possibly the product of a mid-life crisis but more likely his restlessness was caused by the same thing which eventually drove Pearce to crime. An unhealthy combination of anger and ego. He always thought he was better than everyone else and couldn't see why no-one else could see it too. He had his career mapped out in his mind — sergeant, then inspector, chief inspector, command of his own squad and so on. Rodney Whitchelo, Golden Boy of the force. Only it didn't happen like that. He was a good policeman, nothing less, but nothing more. So every step of the fantasy plan that did not succeed was another slap in the face for him and yet another confirmation that the world was passing him by. Of course, it was everyone's fault but his own. He justified this by convincing himself that he had been denied promotion because he was not a Freemason.

In July, 1986, as Whitchelo was pondering his future — and what to do with it — fate tipped in his direction. Whatever his personal misgivings about his career, the impression he gave to colleagues was still that of the diligent officer. His superiors decided that Whitchelo should be sent on a specialist course to learn the latest advanced surveillance techniques. Part of the course was a case study of a blackmail attempt which had been successfully foiled the year before following a complex covert police surveillance operation. As he sat in the lecture room, and listened to his tutors outlining the case, a light went on inside Whitchelo's head.

The case concerned William Frary, who was caught blackmailing Bernard Matthew, the turkey farm millionaire. Frary wanted money paid into a number of accounts he'd set up under false names, or he'd inject poison into Matthew's products on the supermarket shelves. He planned to withdraw the money through cashpoints. Frary had gambled correctly that there would be too many machines for the police to keep surveillance on. But he failed to think his plan through, collecting the cash from a narrow selection of machines in a particular area, enabling police to get a lock on him. At Frary's trial, the judge considered the fine details of the plan were so sophisticated and revealing, he refused to allow them to be published.

Whitchelo, of course, got to learn every detail.

He saw the simple brilliance of the plan and he saw its weaknesses. He saw his way out of the police force and a way into the life he felt he was owed.

Whitchelo returned from that course a changed man. He immediately set about the task of designing the perfect blackmail crime, opening numerous accounts under false names and addresses. Over the next two years, Whitchelo honed his plan, checking and double checking the details. Like Frary's scheme, his was going to be a product contamination blackmail. He took his time, researching poisons, experimenting with different products and packaging to decide which ones he could tamper with undetected. He also set about selecting his victim. He chose Pedigree Pet Foods.

Contact was made in the *Daily Telegraph* personals. The company was to use the code names 'John' and 'Sandra' — 'John' was Pedigree, 'Sandra' was Whitchelo. A phone number was to be set up, which Whitchelo would use, identifying himself with the code words 'Romeo' and 'Juliet'. Whitchelo had also ordered the company not to contact the police, an instruction they ignored. The first message was placed on August 31, 1988.

SANDRA, happy birthday darling. Want to help. Love John

Shortly afterwards Whitchelo made his first call. Between October 28 and December 19, Pedigree deposited £52,000 into his accounts. During this time, communications continued between Pedigree and Whitchelo. Things didn't always go smoothly though. On December 7, an advert appeared in the *Telegraph* after one of Whitchelo's demand letters got delayed.

SANDRA haven't heard from you. Local postal strike. Nothing getting through. Please write or phone. Love John.

The day before Pedigree placed this advert, Whitchelo had strolled into a supermarket in Basildon, Essex, and slipped a doctored can of Pedigree Chum onto the shelf. The food inside was contaminated with salicylic acid. To ensure the tin was found and the metal behind his threat recognised, Whitchelo had marked the tin 'contaminated'. He did this in all the fifteen subsequent cases of poisoning against Pedigree attributed to him.

On December 9 another advert appeared in the *Telegraph*'s personals.

SANDRA letter now arrived. Thanks. Can now meet where you said. Trying hard to help, but only you can make it work at your end. Remember it's just our secret or it has to be all over. Love John

The message was meant to make Whitchelo feel confident the company was playing the game to his rules, whereas in fact, the whole operation was being orchestrated by a specialist police team.

The contaminations continued. At the same time, Whitchelo began withdrawing money from his accounts in sums of £300 per day. He had learned well from the Frary case and used machines all over the country, rarely returning to the same place. Withdrawals were made as far apart as Glasgow, Kings Lynn and Southampton and he wore a crash helmet when taking the money to make sure security cameras outside the building societies and inside the cashpoint machines would not catch an image of his face.

But the key factor in his success was the fact that his own police squad were involved in the hunt for the Pedigree blackmailer. As he was privy to all the tactical strategy decisions being made in the investigation, it was easy for him to stay one step ahead. So confident was he of his ability to outwit his fellow officers, he stepped up the pressure on Pedigree, increasing his demand to £1.25 million.

Things didn't all go Whitchelo's way though. Police computer experts had doctored the computers in the cash machines to process Whitchelo's cash card transactions much slower than a normal withdrawal. The programme they implanted in the system meant that each time Whitchelo entered his PIN number, the machines would take progressively longer to pay out. The plan was that if Whitchelo was withdrawing money from machines in a surveillance area, the stalling programme would delay him long enough for police to flood the area with officers. But as Whitchelo knew which cash machines would be under surveillance and when and altered his plans accordingly, so the delay programme was nothing more than an irritant for him. The thing that really did frustrate Whitchelo though, was Pedigree's stalling tactics. Money was drip fed into the accounts and only topped up at the last possible minute. Also, the police began to close Whitchelo's accounts one by one, until the last was shut down on March 28, 1989. By this time, Whitchelo had managed to withdraw £18,000.

Earlier that year, Whitchelo had gone on sick leave from his squad suffering from asthma. In March 1989 he retired from the force on medical grounds, telling his colleagues he was going to set up a computer firm. He did indeed set the firm up, but it was not a success and eventually collapsed. Although a disappointment for Whitchelo, the failure of his business was not a disaster. He had decided his real interest was blackmail and set about making it a profitable full-time career. With his campaign against Pedigree now stagnant, Whitchelo reviewed his tactics and chose a new victim. This time, he went for the jugular, targeting a company whose customers were the most vulnerable of all — children.

Whitchelo homed in on Heinz baby food. He knew how sensitive the company would be to an attack in this area, correctly reasoning that there would be mass panic if families thought their children could be poisoned. Heinz, he thought, were bound to pay up quickly rather than see their products swept off supermarket shelves and their brand name destroyed. When Whitchelo made the decision to switch targets, he vowed he'd go in hard from day one. His letters to Heinz spelt this out in no uncertain terms.

Heinz will be irreversibly ruined after their entire product range has been attacked with the most lethal substances and boycotted by the public. There will have been many casualties before we have finished with them.

A follow-up letter was chilling:

An infant's death will be another statistic as far as we are concerned, but will ensure that we are not ignored. We will continue until there is public uproar and further massive publicity.

94

Welcome to the Mardi Gra Experience

Using his knowledge of forensic techniques, Whitchelo wrote his letters on paper which was widely available and then photocopied them so there would be no fingerprints or other forensic evidence. In total, Whitchelo's letters demanded £2.5 million from Heinz.

To back up his threats, he embarked on an intensive poisoning campaign, spiking not just baby food, but soup, baked beans, sandwich spread and ketchup. He also contacted newspapers, supermarkets and even police stations with details of where he had left poisoned tins. By the end of June 1989, the whole country knew about the blackmail campaign and were deserting Heinz products in their droves. The panic intensified after a nine-month-old baby was fed broken glass and razor blades that had been placed in a tub of yoghurt. Only the quick action of the baby's mother saved the child from serious injury. Other substances used by Whitchelo included pesticides and caustic soda. One jar of baby food contained enough caustic soda to kill 27 children.

Baby food manufacturers who were not being targeted by Whitchelo were also caught up in the scare. A wave of copycat contaminations ensued; at one stage more than 1,000 incidents a day were being reported. Virtually every one of them was bogus, perpetrated by parents trying to cash in, hoping the companies would send them vouchers or money in compensation. One baby food firm, Cow & Gate, was forced to remove 100 million jars of baby food from sale and destroy them at a cost of £32 million.

Meanwhile, Heinz — despite losing millions themselves — refused to pay up. In a terse message published in the *Telegraph*, Whitchelo read:

SANDRA. Now that you have changed the rules, Bob [the police] is involved and says we can no longer meet or write. John.

The company then offered a £100,000 reward for the capture of the blackmailer. And Whitchelo, ever the opportunist, made an audacious move. If he couldn't get the money directly from blackmail, he would get it indirectly — by claiming his own reward money. On September 5, 1989, he wrote to Heinz saying he knew the identity of the blackmailer, but was scared to reveal it straight away because the blackmailer was a 'bent cop'. Instead, he asked for £50,000 to be paid into eight new building society accounts in the name of Ian and Nina Fox. The details of the accounts were then sent to dozens of bogus accommodation addresses set up by Whitchelo. A new police operation, Operation Stab, was set up to monitor these addresses, but yet again Whitchelo was able to evade capture and start milking the accounts of money.

How he was able to do this, despite now being retired from the police, was something that was to cause great embarrassment to the police when the case eventually came to court.

The police force is a tight-knit community. Even when an officer has left the force, close contact is retained with old colleagues. Whitchelo ensured he stayed in touch with his friends still serving on the Regional Crime Squad. During his trial, the court was told how he obtained sensitive information from unsuspecting friends over drinks and was even invited to the investigating team's Christmas party. However, in an interview for this book, a detective who worked on the case has claimed Whitchelo's involvement with the squad after his retirement was a much deeper one than has previously been admitted.

The officer, who has asked not to be named, claims, 'Whitchelo was great with computers. He set up his own computer company and attended the Yard's regular computer club meetings. After he left, he continued to stay in touch, but it wasn't just chit-chat about old times. He was actually providing help with the computer systems we were using in the operation. It was all off the record, but nevertheless he was there to help them with the set up of their computers while asking how the enquiry was going. They told him which cashpoints they were covering.'

If this is true, it meant that Whitchelo was actually influencing the investigation against him. Combine this with all the extra information he gleaned about the operation and it's no wonder he was invisible to the police.

Operation Stab was getting nowhere and the blackmail campaign had now begun to affect the country at the very highest level. Heinz had become so concerned about the way in which the blackmailer was able to evade capture it feared it was only a matter of time before the company was damaged beyond repair. In America, the company's top executives drew up a top secret plan to close down its entire UK operation and move it abroad. The plan reached the ears of Margaret Thatcher, who immediately summoned the then Home Secretary, Douglas Hurd. In an unprecedented personal intervention, Mrs Thatcher told Hurd to spare no expense in catching the baby food blackmailer. A former senior Metropolitan police officer has told me that Mrs Thatcher personally ordered the transfer of £8 million from the Home Office to the Met's Specialist Operations Department. 'That money paid off our departmental overspend, and more than financed the current operation. It also persuaded Heinz not to carry out its threat', revealed the officer, who then admitted, 'If we'd been working within the original budget, we'd still be trying to work this case out.'

When Whitchelo bid for the reward money, the police finally made the inevitable, awful, connection that had so far eluded them — that the blackmailer was one of their own. In his letter to Heinz, Whitchelo had revealed information about the operation only a policeman could know. He even named officers working on the case.

Detective Chief Superintendent Pat Fleming was in day-to-day command of the investigation at the time. If the blackmailer was a policeman, Fleming knew that nothing he nor his 45 strong-squad did would make any difference. But if he shut down the investigation, the blackmailer would be tipped off that something was wrong and disappear. He decided the only way to catch the blackmailer was to set up a parallel 'virtual' investigation. This would shadow the original squad, which would be sent unknowingly on dummy operations to watch cashpoint machines in one area. The 'virtual' squad would then mount surveillance on the real target area. Fleming hoped that if the blackmailer was getting his information from his original squad, he would walk into the trap believing the police surveillance teams were miles away from where he was operating.

Only Fleming's boss, Deputy Assistant Commissioner

Welcome to the Mardi Gra Experience

Simon Crawshaw, and three other trusted officers knew about the new plan, code-named Operation Agincourt. To man the 'virtual' enquiry, 40 officers from Special Branch were drafted in. And even they weren't told what was really going on.

Under the police's instructions, Heinz paid £16,000 into two accounts at the Woolwich and Nationwide building societies. Cashpoints in the Home Counties were targeted by the new squad, which settled down into what was to become a marathon surveillance operation.

Five weeks later, nearly all the money was gone from the accounts. Despite feeding false information through the original squad, the blackmailer had managed to evade capture. The Met were becoming desperate.

On Friday 13, October, the Agincourt officers embarked on a final attempt to catch the blackmailer. Fifteen Woolwich cash machines in and around London were identified and placed under 24-hour surveillance. Using specially linked computers, the machines would instantly tell the team which machine was being used and officers would move in from their hiding places. Choosing just fifteen machines was a big risk. There are thousands of cashpoints in London and Whitchelo could have used any of them. But the team had nothing left to lose.

Seven days later, on the night of October 20, the operation was still running. Foul weather had brought chaos to London and to the team. Power lines supplying banks and building societies had been brought down, knocking out cashpoints across the city. It seemed unlikely the blackmailer would show. But it was decided to keep the operation going for a few hours more just in case. And with the power down, Special Branch were just going to have to rely on gut instinct.

It was a terrible night, cold and hammering down with rain. The surveillance team were just about to shut down the night when just after midnight a car drove up to a Woolwich cash machine in Enfield. The man got out of his car wearing a crash helmet. One officer followed him to the machine, but when the man got there he saw it was out of order and turned back. As he was walking back to the car, he was grabbed.

It was Whitchelo.

Detective Sergeant John Kerton was there when they apprehended him. He recalled what happened next. 'I said to Mr Whitchelo, "What's the crash helmet for?" He stammered something about it protecting him from the rain.' The officers searched Whitchelo's car and found building society cards in the names of Ian and Nina Fox. When Whitchelo was read his rights, he replied, 'No problem guys, I know what this is about, but I'm innocent.' Then he fainted. Back at Operation Agincourt's HQ, the message Pat Fleming had spent months waiting for came through.

'Got the target.'

When detectives went to search his home, they were confronted by a sticker bearing the picture of a fierce-looking Alsation dog and the words I LIVE HERE. But like so many things in Whitchelo's life, what lay behind was far removed from the image that was presented. Officers were greeted by nothing more savage than a yapping poodle. Once past this formidable guard dog, they proceeded to tear the house apart for evidence, finding drills, caustic soda, a portable telephone, a syringe bearing traces of poison and a typewriter whose key strokes matched those used in the blackmail letters.

But if the jubilant officers thought Whitchelo was just going to roll over once faced with all the incontrovertible evidence against him, they were to be disappointed. What came out of Whitchelo's mouth next was described by one officer as 'One of the best fairy stories since the Brothers Grimm'. It was a story Whitchelo was to stick to until the bitter end and which would be aired during his Old Bailey trial which began in October 1990. When he finally appeared in the dock, Whitchelo pled not guilty to a total of eighteen charges; six of blackmail, four of contaminating goods with intent, two of obtaining property by deception, one of threatening to kill, one intent to cause grievous bodily harm with a razor blade and four charges of placing corrosive substances in products with intent to cause grievous bodily harm.

According to Whitchelo, he wasn't the blackmailer at all. He was in fact working for the police on an ultra-secret undercover mission. Whitchelo said he had been recruited by two of his former colleagues, Detective Sergeant Stephen Hobbs and Detective Chief Inspector Gavin Robertson, who had come to his house in October 1988 to ask for his help in flushing out the extortionist. Whitchelo said the two detectives told him they suspected the blackmailer was a senior policeman on the Operation Stab investigating team and needed someone from the outside to work on the case. As Whitchelo had just retired and had been on the special blackmail course, he would be perfect for the job. His role would be to replace the blackmailer's original accomplice, known only as 'Lynne', who had become a registered police informant. Whitchelo was to take over from her withdrawing the money from building society cashpoints and then deposit the cash into another account. The plan was that Whitchelo would make the withdrawals but not the deposits, thereby forcing the blackmailer to come and seek out 'Lynne', who would be under surveillance. 'It seemed perfectly plausible', Whitchelo was to later tell an Old Bailey jury.

Whitchelo continued to embroider further details into his tale. The crash helmet had been provided by DCI Robertson to avoid him being recognised by the corrupt officer if he was caught on security cameras. He'd been given a certificate stating he was working undercover for the police. He was also given the building society cash cards and a pager. He had proof he said, in his diary and in an electronic organiser where he had kept notes of his meeting with the two detectives. When asked where they all were, he said the diary and certificate had 'gone missing' after the police search and the Psion's memory had been wiped because the police had let its batteries run flat. Because of this, he argued, the real blackmailers must be DCI Robertson and DS Hobbs.

'It never crossed my mind that I was being made a patsy,' he pleaded.

It was all lies of course, just like all the other lies Whitchelo had told about interviewing the Queen and infiltrating the IRA. Those lies along with many others were exposed as one after another, witnesses stood up in court to reveal the real Rodney Whitchelo.

The real Rodney Whitchelo who liked to be whipped by prostitutes until he bled. Whitchelo's craving for this kind of sex led him to try and set up his own kinky club, The Sadists and Masochists Pen Pal Club, where like-minded people could meet and exchange fantasies. The club was a total flop, attracting just four subscribers, all of them men. But it was Whitchelo's leanings in this area which was to provide some of the most damning evidence against him. After meeting one woman via a sex contact magazine, Whitchelo used a cashpoint near hotel where they had enjoyed an afternoon together. After a second such meeting, another withdrawal was made from a cashpoint near to the hotel they had used. Detectives were also able to trace phone calls made by Whitchelo on his mobile phone to within yards of other machines money had been taken from.

Whitchelo's ex-fiancée, told how he had talked about committing the perfect crime. He also warned her not to feed her dog Pedigree Chum, claiming he had 'inside knowledge' of the extortion bid. One time he had even blurted out that he was the blackmailer, but upon seeing her shocked reaction had pretended it was a joke.

Whitchelo's tendency to try and show everyone how clever he was by skating dangerously close to the edge of his reality was demonstrated in breathtaking manner about half way through the trial. The prosecution called as a witness George Webber, a former *Daily Mirror* journalist who had met Whitchelo after Fagin's Buckingham Palace break in. Webber told the court that Whitchelo had become a good contact and eventually a friend. After Whitchelo had retired from the police, he approached Webber to ask him to ghost write a crime novel about the perfect crime. The book, claimed Whitchelo, would expose all the loopholes in the law he as a police officer thought should be shut. The book, said Whitchelo, would centre on a sophisticated blackmail plot and show how elite criminals got away with their crimes. During a taped interview with Webber, Whitchelo had even given details of how not getting caught.

It was hardly surprising when, after hearing ten weeks of damning evidence, the jury found him guilty on eleven counts. Sentencing him, Judge Nina Lowry said, 'Blackmail on such a scale as this inevitably affects large sections of the community, causing grave anxiety and untold economic loss from food manufacturing industries . . . You hoped by using methods learnt as a detective you could escape arrest . . . By choosing babies you picked the most vulnerable section of the community. You expected to strike terror into the minds of the public and force Heinz to pay up.'

She sentenced Whitchelo to seventeen years in prison. He showed no emotion as he was sentenced, and was led away to start a prison term which would be, according to his barrister, 'a living hell'. As an ex-policeman and someone who had threatened babies, he would be a natural target for vengeful cons.

After the trial, one of the men Whitchelo had falsely accused — DCI Gavin Robertson — summed up the feelings of the entire team, 'The worst thing about this whole thing is the gross betrayal of his friends and ex-colleagues. The damage this has done to the reputation of the police service is unforgivable.'

For Roy Ramm, still trying to work out who was behind Mardi Gra, the spectre of Whitchelo loomed large. 'Whitchelo was a real shock for the Met. Once it was thought that it could be a police officer can you imagine the number of people that were under suspicion?' Whitchelo's betrayal is something that will never be forgotten in the Met, and certainly never forgiven.

That damage was to force the Mardi Gra team to consider the possibility, however remote, that the blackmailer could again be one of their own. They had learned from the Witchelo case, but had they learned well enough?

At the forefront in their minds was the incredible possibility that Whitchelo could be behind the Mardi Gra Experience. Whitchelo was still in prison when the bombings started, but what if he'd been talking about what he did and how he did it? It's often said that prisons are universities of crime. What if someone had been taking a few lessons either directly, or indirectly?

Sources close to Operation Heath have indicated that they took this possibility seriously enough to undertake covert surveillance on a number of men who were known to have had close contact with Whitchelo while he was in jail.

As we now know, Whitchelo had absolutely nothing to do with the Mardi Gra Experience, other than to have provided a source of inspiration for Pearce. This is Whitchelo's legacy — the 'untold commercial damage' judge Lowry identified as being left in Whitchelo's wake. It is damage which continues to have effect today and whose trail was picked up by Edgar Pearce just four years after Whitchelo was sent to prison.

Pearce was inspired by the man.

But he knew he could do better.

Go that one important stage further.

Win.

A New Target

Welcome to the Mardi Gra Experience

In the two months that followed his gas cylinder bomb attack on the Eltham branch of Barclays, Pearce spent his time developing and building further prototypes in his greenhouse bomb factory, then testing them in a remote field far away from prying eyes. The fact that Pearce went to such lengths to ensure the viability of his devices reveals his total determination to achieve his ends by causing actual harm. Detective Chief Superintendent Jeffery Rees — who eventually captured Pearce — believes this fact alone should be enough to dispel any thought that Pearce was simply an eccentric old man with some quirky grudges. Many press reports stated that most of Pearce's devices had been designed not to fire. This, assert the police, is not the case. Nearly all Pearce's bombs were sent or delivered fully working. It was only Pearce's lack of true bomb-making skills that saved a lot of lives. Pearce was obviously aware of this, hence the research. He was identifying the faults in his work and making the necessary changes, a pattern of learning he was keen the police should pick up on.

He also spent the time reconsidering his strategy. Despite the lines of communication opened up by Barclays, Pearce had resisted all invitations to engage in further dialogue with the company, suspecting correctly that the police were behind the move. He knew that if the police were behind the adverts, supporting and advising Barclays, then his leverage against the bank would be weakened. So he directed his thinking towards ways in which he could increase the amount of pressure he could exert on the bank. He came back to the situation he had found himself in the summer when, because of a lack of media coverage, he had been forced to bomb his own local. That experience had convinced him the police were holding back news of the attacks. Pearce therefore decided to publicise his campaign himself. After all, he was an advertising expert. If the mountain wouldn't come to Mohammed . . .

On an electronic typewriter, he bashed out a 'press release' outlining his campaign and accusing the bank and the police of endangering the lives of customers by covering up the danger he posed. Avoiding the *Telegraph*, who he now saw as police collaborators, Pearce chose the *Daily Mail* and enclosed a little extra something to ram home his point — a Polaroid picture of his latest device. On April 3, 1996, the following letter was opened at the *Daily Mail* offices:

Mardi Gra — a gripping story of a cover up. Mardi Gra is the codename [sic] of a small group of Barclays bank victims, who are in the process of reversing the tide of fortune into their favour. After a year of activity, more than 25 devices of variable intensity have been deployed. Previously, our earlier devices were designed as frighteners to demonstrate political will, ability to strike and access to a constant supply of explosive material. We are amazed that a bank appears not to care who gets injured by persuading the police to keep quiet about it. The enclosed stat is of our latest device. Essentially it is an 18 inch barrel double-barrelled 12-gauge shotgun with a now totally perfect bolt firing mechanism and a cunningly designed timed firing release that delays the second discharge. The targets will be Barclay customers going to or from a bank, cashpoint and or followed home for residential strikes . . . The time limit is seven days for an item of value to appear in the *Mail*.

Pearce's reasons for choosing the *Daily Mail* to be the recipient of his 'outing'? 'I sent it to the *Daily Mail* to see if there were any press restrictions,' he confessed later. 'I chose the *Mail* because of sympathetic item regarding a cover up about a small company being stretched by a big company.' Here's Pearce again, playing the victim, the wronged little man fighting the unjust big organisation.

The paper handed over the letter and photograph to the police. If the letter was genuine, they were sitting on a hot story, one that they had become a part of. The paper was anxious to have the details confirmed. The police and Barclays were now faced with a dilemma. The strategy had been to force the blackmailer into making a mistake by keeping him in the dark. Now that he had short-circuited that strategy, it would only be a matter of time before the story began to leak out. The team had no choice. They went public.

At a packed press conference Detective Superintendent John Beadle of Specialist Operations did his best to limit the damage that would inevitably be caused by the revelation of the bombing campaign. 'I must stress that the real threat to the public is low. The fear of crime is much greater that the reality . . . My advice is to report anything suspicious to the police, but the public should carry on their normal daily lives,' he urged.

The media responded to the urge for calm with unrestrained enthusiasm. Double page spreads, chronicling Mardi Gra's campaign to date and describing the construction and potential of his devices, were everywhere. Television and radio news teams leapt on the story.

Pearce was delighted. In his front room den he toasted his success with more red wine and sat glued to the sofa watching the bulletins, reading and re-reading the newspaper articles. At last, a victory! He had bent Barclays and the police to his will. This was the defining moment. He knew that he now had to capitalise on his advantage. He began work on assembling the shotgun device he had described to the *Daily Mail*.

April 20, Pearce placed a black plastic bin liner in an alleyway adjacent to Barclays bank at Ealing Broadway, in west London. Inside lurked the boasted-about 'shotgun' device. It wasn't actually a shotgun, but a more sophisticated version of Pearce's first video box design. Only now, Pearce had added a single home-made barrel to act as a compression chamber to give the shot in the Winchester brand clay pigeon cartridge greater force and better direction. The firing mechanism was linked to a clockwork timer. It went off as planned at 3.00 p.m. The bag ripped open and a split second later three people standing a few yards away were peppered with shotgun pellets travelling at over 300 feet per second. For the first time since December 6th, 1994, a Mardi Gra device had caused actual harm. The media were quickly on the scene, capturing footage of the injured being taken away by ambulance crews.

The new power Pearce had brought to his bombs and the injuries caused were an alarming escalation. He'd obviously been emboldened by his sudden fame and as police had originally feared when they imposed the news blackout, was beginning to feed off his notoriety. It looked as though things were going to get very bad.

But instead, something very odd happened.

Since his accident in 1992, Pearce had been a compulsive watcher of television. Now that he was a 'star', his viewing took on new meaning and significance — monitoring the channels for news about himself. One day, Pearce was watching a BBC news broadcast about his campaign. The interviewee in that story was Barclays Chairman Andrew Buxton, who revealed that Barclays was preparing to take drastic steps to protect itself. 'Including closing branches down?' asked the interviewer. 'If that was necessary then yes, we would do it,' the chairman replied.

The interview stopped Pearce in his tracks. His reaction to it revealed the contradictory and disorganised thinking that lay underneath his apparent determination. After nearly eighteen months of activity, Pearce decided simply to stop.

In his post-arrest interviews, he said of his change of heart, 'The Barclays episode finished when the chief executive came on TV. I didn't want them to close banks simply because I was bombing them.'

This explanation makes no sense for two reasons. Firstly, surely this was exactly the kind of thing he wanted to happen and had been working towards? Barclays, by admitting they were considering branch closures as a result of the Mardi Gra campaign, were very publicly showing the extreme pressure they were under. Pearce's aim all along had been to keep at them until they buckled. Secondly, are we really expected to believe that Pearce was quite content to blow up Barclays staff and customers, but balked at the idea of a few branches being closed down?

And yet there he was, probably closer to a result than he had ever been, deciding to back off. His police statement is either a lie, which is unlikely given the extraordinarily frank confession he made, or he is actually telling the truth and thereby revealing a mind that is beginning to lose its ability to hold together consistent patterns of thought and logic. Yet again, everything about Pearce's campaign is strange and off kilter. He is the blackmailer who doesn't respond to messages he has ordered; the blackmailer who asks for money and then makes no effort to collect.

Despite having decided to call off his campaign against Barclays, Pearce had by no means decided to abandon his plans for blackmail. He did, after all, have the plan for the perfect blackmail, one which would provide him with all the money he would ever need to enjoy a comfortable old age. It was just a matter of finding the right target . . .

And again it was the television, the thing Pearce feared he was doomed to spend the rest of his life slumped before, that provided him with an answer and showed him the way.

Of all the battles fought by businesses to win the money in our pockets, none have been so fierce as those between supermarkets. After decimating independent High Street traders through the 1980s with their superstores and out-of-town developments, the supermarkets then turned on each other. The top two players in the supermarket game, Tesco and Sainsbury's, are locked in such competition to be number one that their rivalry has become so heated it makes national news. Sainsbury's had held the coveted number one position for years until 1995 when arch-rival Tesco toppled them from the throne. This usurpation was widely carried on news programmes and across newspaper pages. Someone who took more interest than most was Edgar Pearce.

'If Sainsbury's were really struggling in a battle against Tesco,' Pearce said at interview, 'the last thing they'd want would be people boycotting their shops because of the threat of bombs. It seemed logical they would want to meet the demands.'

On the July 10, 1996 a Mardi Gra demand letter arrived at Sainsbury's head office in central London.

Welcome to the Mardi Gra Experience . . . The police will be able to fill in the general details of the deal as we are almost old chums . . . You have seven days to respond followed by a death or glory outcome. Now there's a deal that's a boardroom winner!

In the communiqué, Pearce also made it clear that his Barclays respite was not indefinite. He would, he warned, be coming back for them at some stage.

This switch of targets hit Operation Heath hard. It had been difficult enough trying to trawl through the list of possible suspects who might have a grudge against Barclays. But now they would have to go back and start all over again, cross-checking databases for people with grudges against Barclays and Sainsbury's. It was, of course, a futile exercise because there was nothing there to find.

As with Barclays, the police responded to Pearce's demand in the personal columns, this time in the *Daily Mail*, it for the moment seeming to be his preferred newspaper for clandestine communications.

MARDI GRA We are ready to help and give value. Contact us on the verification number

Silence. Nothing.

Mardi Gra had gone to ground again, this time for five months. But this superficial inactivity hid a period of intense review and plotting. Buoyed by the press coverage Pearce decided to concentrate on what he called 'his PR campaign'. The way to generate massive pressure on Sainsbury's would be to build up greater media coverage. To do this, he hit on the idea of threatening to pre-select individual Sainsbury's customers as targets. Between the end of July and the beginning of December that year, Pearce stalked various branches in London and the Home Counties armed with a camera. He took more than one hundred photographs of lone women shoppers. These photographs were then marked on the back with labels which read 'targeted for action'. One picture had 'Hit No 5' written on the back. He carefully filed these photographs away in envelopes and waited for the right time to activate the next part of his new plan.

Pearce wanted to ensure he attacked Sainsbury's when they would be particularly vulnerable to a sudden drop in business. Mid-December would be perfect — the start of the peak Christmas shopping period and a time when most companies look to take in a day what they normally take in a week. The waiting game Pearce played here again reveals how he was resigned to a long campaign of attrition. What were a few months of inactivity compared to the lifetime of bounty he was looking forward to, when every day he would be able to reap the fruits of his labours from cash machines all over the country?

On December 17, Pearce sat in his front room, leafing through the sheaves of photographs. As always, he was wearing gloves and after choosing a picture, slid it into an envelope together with a new demand note. The envelope was addressed not to Sainsbury's, but to the *Daily Mail*. The accompanying demand said that unless the supermarket paid up, Mardi Gra was going to start shooting Sainsbury's customers with a crossbow. Despite Pearce's interview assertion that this stage of the extortion was a 'PR campaign', and thereby inferring his threats were somehow more benign or in some way less serious, the crossbow attacks were no an idle threat. Pearce had purchased two crossbows and had manufactured around a dozen arrows himself. After sawing off the stock to make the crossbows shorter, he adapted a large Sainsbury's carrier bag, giving it a reinforced bottom and cutting a slit in the side. A crossbow was mounted inside the bag on the base, with the arrow's tip facing the slit. Fishing wire was attached to the trigger, running out through the back of the bag. Pearce's tactic would be to mingle with a busy crowd of shoppers in front of a Sainsbury's store, the loaded crossbow concealed in the bag. He could then fire into the crowd using the fishing wire to pull the trigger and be walking away from the havoc he had caused a fraction of a second later. In a panic-stricken crowd of people carrying identical shopping bags, he could strike unnoticed and escape with ease. There was no doubt about it. The crossbows were built to kill.

For some reason, Pearce did not carry out this threat, probably because this kind of attack would have required him to be present at the moment of impact. If he was there when he fired, he would be there to hear the screams and that wasn't part of his game. He liked to attack remotely and in safety, snugly hidden away from the noise, mess and human consequences of his actions. The crossbows were built to kill but they were used as a bluff.

The Met called his bluff. At the investigating team's request the *Daily Mail* did not publish the photograph.

Christmas came and went. On January 7, 1997, Pearce tried again, sending two more photographs to the newspaper together with one of his home-made crossbow bolts. Again, the paper withheld the pictures. Pearce knew that the police had got to the newspaper.

The failure of this tactic clearly affected Pearce and made him question the fundamental nature of the way he was going about his blackmail attempt. He'd been active now for just over two years and not one penny had come his way. He was deeply puzzled that the plan itself simply wasn't working. Just as Commander Roy Ramm predicted, Pearce had scripted his plan to the last detail. He would send his bombs, then he would make his threats and the companies would pay up. But the companies weren't following the script. It seemed that, somewhere along the way, everyone had forgotten their lines.

Pearce needed to find a way to get things moving again and to ensure that when he did come out, he was safe and anonymous. So he retreated again.

Pearce was to disappear for nearly eleven months. During the quiet period police were wondering what had happened to the bomber. When there are gaps in an offending pattern, one common explanation is that the perpetrator is in prison for another crime. Was Mardi Gra serving time for something else? Or maybe he had been admitted to a mental hospital? He was obviously unstable, reasoned the police, so it was a possibility.

Wherever he was and whatever he was doing, Operation Heath continued. The team knew that Mardi Gra would be back and they weren't going to wait for him to make next his move. New ideas had to be pursued, new leads tracked down.

Profiling High and Low

Welcome to the Mardi Gra Experience

On the same day that Mardi Gra was unmasking himself to the *Daily Mail* in England, over in America the Federal Bureau of Investigation were making an arrest that would bring to an end the reign of a bomber who had terrorised the country for seventeen years.

In Britain, many people were beginning to draw attention to the apparent similarities between the two cases. Like Mardi Gra, this bomber had struck randomly and without warning. Like Mardi Gra, this bomber had managed to avoid being detected despite a huge investigation by the FBI.

Unlike Mardi Gra so far, he had killed people.

Casting their eyes across the Atlantic, the Met could only pray that Mardi Gra was caught before he followed in the bloody footsteps of The Unabomber.

When Theodore Kaczynski stood up in court he pleaded guilty to the murder of three completely innocent people and injuring 23 others. He was, he confessed, the notorious 'Unabomber', one-man fighter against 'the system.'

Because serial bombers are extremely rare, Operation Heath investigators were naturally interested in the case. They feared the Unabomer would prove to be some sort of inspiration to Pearce. But they hoped the parallels might help track him down. Either way, they needed all the information they could get to draw up a bigger, and clearer, picture of the sort of man they were dealing with.

From an early age, Ted Kaczynski was reclusive. A mathematics prodigy at school, he grew up feeling himself to be a social outcast. Like Pearce, he tried to let his talents take him into situations where he could succeed and find direction. Like Pearce, he failed. He could never see anything through to completion, he couldn't use his genius positively. It was a burden. It weighed him down with expectation rather than setting him free. He took prestigious academic positions then left abruptly. In the early 70s the world became just too much for him to cope with and he dropped out altogether, holing up in a log cabin in the Montana woodlands, hatching his version of revenge.

Kaczynski had become obsessed with technology. Or, as he saw it, the way technology and those who propagated it were destroying the world. He felt it was his duty to reverse the trend. Geneticists, industrialists, big business. Anyone linked with discovering, promoting or researching new technology would be fair game for his deadly packages.

Like Pearce, he enjoyed the correspondence, the toying with the media and his targets. But Kaczynski's diatribes made Pearce's seem tame in comparison. This is an extract from a letter sent to his fourteenth victim:

Dr Gelernter: 'People with advanced degrees aren't as smart as they think they are. If you'd had any brains you would have realised that there are a lot of people out there who bitterly resent the way techno-nerds like you are changing the world and you wouldn't have been dumb enough to open an unexpected package from an unknown source.'

The letter continued in an incoherent, violently angry and merciless polemic, criticising Gelernter for stating in a book that the advance of computerisation was 'inevitable'. At least Gelernter knew why he had been targeted. At least there was method in the madness. Pearce, on the other hand, revelled in randomness.

Kaczynski took satisfaction from the body count. Bombs which left people maimed were 'producing good results', he wrote in his diary, but also complained they were not deadly enough. He openly discussed his desire to 'start killing people' although on the same page wrote of his concern that people would see him as a 'sickie'.

Kaczynski, it should be noted, was diagnosed paranoid schizophrenic. Pearce clearly wasn't in that league — yet. Though the investigating team weren't to know it at the time, there were big parallels. The sense of failure, of wasted talent, of not linking with the world around them, a bitterness that ate at the very heart of their soul.

Kaczynski believed in killing. Pearce wanted to be recognised, and if that meant people getting hurt, so be it. They shouldn't get in the way.

The Met could also learn from the logistical difficulties of such a long-running, widespread case. In the seventeen years Kaczynski spent bombing America nearly every one of the FBI's 56 field divisions had been involved at some time or another in the investigation. Around 2,500 suspects had been investigated; 22,000 pages of documentary evidence assembled; 8,000 exhibits collected; 82 million items of data sifted through.

After the guilty verdict, FBI Director Louis Freeh said, 'The search for the Unabomber was one of the longest-running, most difficult, most frustrating cases in the history of the FBI or any law enforcement agency.'

These were words the Met back in London could sympathise with. Frustrating. Difficult. *Long-running*.

'The FBI sympathises with the loved ones of those who were killed and with those who were injured in the bombings. We regret that we did not catch the Unabomber sooner.' Another sentence which resonated close to the heart of Operation Heath. The team felt it was only a matter of time before Mardi Gra finally managed to kill someone, whether he intended to or not. None of them wanted to face the day when they would have to apologise to the family of Mardi Gra's first fatality.

Professor Bill Tafoya was the lead profiler with the FBI's Unabomber Task Force. In 1993, he produced a profile of the perpetrator which proved to be uncannily accurate. The Met were keen to draw on his expertise in the Mardi Gra case.

He agreed willingly. 'Mardi Gra,' he wrote, 'may have been insulted by a checkout girl or a bag boy. He may have bought a bad chicken from Sainsbury's. It could be that simple.' Or maybe he had had a credit card application turned down by Barclaycard. In other words, it could be anything.

Whoever he was, Tafoya argued, he was likely to be of

normal intelligence, with a boring or menial job and harbour a real grudge. He would feel 'undervalued', that he had 'not got his just reward from life'. He would dress in a boring manner and live in London, possibly in one of its poorer areas. 'I think this guy is probably a loner. He's not going to be in the limelight.'

Looking at the devices sent by Mardi Gra, Tafoya said they suggested that Mardi Gra may be a former serviceman or an engineer. He might belong, or have belonged, to a gun club. 'The Mardi Gra bomber is using unsophisticated devices. He has consistently used shotgun shells to target people. The way he cloaks these devices is fairly clever, but the mechanisms themselves — the explosive devices — are very unsophisticated and take little knowledge to make.'

In this respect, said Tafoya, Mardi Gra should not be compared to the Unabomber. 'Kaczynski's bombs escalated in sophistication. They got smaller and more powerful and required different kinds of igniters, calling on a very specialised kind of knowledge. If Mardi Gra had the intellectual capacity to make more complex bombs, he would have done so by now.'

And what was Mardi Gra's motivation? According to Tafoya, 'He's looking for attention not money — that does not interest him.'

The Met also called on a very different type of profiling to aid their investigation. In 1996, they decided to bring in a Canadian expert in a revolutionary detection system known as geographical profiling, a technique which at the time had only just passed through its experimental stage, and was originally developed to help hunt down serial killers. Detective Inspector Kim Rossmo, was a policeman of sixteen years standing, who had helped pioneer this new breakthrough. While studying part-time for his Ph.D. in criminology, he became convinced that if you looked at where an offender was committing crimes, it should be possible to work out the area where they lived. The theory behind this is that everyone operates within defined routines. Research has revealed that in all areas of life people adhere to remarkable, consistent and subconscious patterns of behaviour. For instance, right-handed people generally run to the left when escaping danger; men who are lost will generally head downhill, while women will go up.

Rossmo was interested in the behaviour patterns set up by everyday life, patterns governed by where people live, work, shop and play. A serial offender will operate within these patterns when active in the same way normal people will when, say, planning a shopping trip. This makes sense, because whenever we plan an activity, it will usually pivot around the location of our homes. Whatever you're doing, where you live will dictate the parameters in which you act. It's all part of a daily pattern of behaviour, a 'life landscape'. The argument goes: if someone becomes a serial offender, they offend within this pattern. Now, though, things get a little more complicated because you have to factor in The Journey to Crime Theory, which states that a criminal will generally not offend within a certain area around his home, mainly because he fears recognition and therefore detection, but also because 'you don't piss on your own doorstep'. This area is marked by 'buffer zones'. Beyond those zones is another area the criminal will also be familiar with and it is here that crimes are most likely to be committed. The further the criminal gets from the outside of his buffer zones, the less likely he is to offend because the surroundings are unfamiliar.

The task Rossmo set about tackling was how to convert all these theories and findings into a workable detection system. This was done by using algorithms which could convert the co-ordinates of crimes and the Journey to Crime Theory into digital maps which pinpoint likely locations of offenders. These maps produce what is known as a 'jeopardy surface', a 3D model in which likely locations appear as red peaks. The bigger and redder the peak, the more likely it is an offender is based within that area.

Rossmo explains, 'Let's just say we are looking at a serial sex offender, who attacks only teenage girls. When you look through the crime database for known offenders you get a list of 2,000 names. After further checking on things like if people on the list are in or out of jail, still alive, still living in the region, you get the list down to 1,000 names. A psychological profile can then get that list down to about 600 names by eliminating all those who don't fit the picture. Now we do the geographic profile. Not only can we input all the locations of the crimes, but we can plug in the addresses of the suspects.' This then highlights those offenders identified by the computer as inhabiting likely locations.

These are the people detectives can then quickly home in on. Does it work? To date, the success rate for geographic profiling has been dramatic, with police arresting an offender named in the top 5% of a list of suspects highlighted on the geographic profile. Rossmo stresses, though, that geographic profiling — like all profiling — is no substitute for traditional human-led crime investigation. It's a tool, not a solution. What it does is help push an inquiry towards a good suspect. 'There are really only three ways you can solve a crime,' says Rossmo. 'Physical evidence, confessions or eye-witnesses. Profiling can help make sense of these or focus an investigation, but it can't solve the crime.'

Invstigators who had been working all hours on

Operation Heath but with little progress, believed geographical profiling could be just the thing to narrow down the possibilities. Putting the random postal bombings between May 19 and July 13, 1995 to one side, the concentration of attacks had been in the west and south east of London, with by far the majority occurring in the west of the city. This clear pattern was obviously one that would be ideally suited to analysis by geographical profiling. 'It was,' says Rossmo, 'a classic case,' for his technique.

Just one month after gaining his doctorate Rossmo was on a plane to England with the prototype profiling software, called Orion, to start on the ground research on the Mardi Gra case. He spent three days visiting the locations of Mardi Gra's 24 attacks so far. 'I had to create a scenario for the computer,' he explains. 'And humans are much better than computers for detecting patterns.' By visiting each scene personally, Rossmo ensured he would be able to make the best possible interpretation of the jeopardy surface that was waiting at the end of the process.

Back in Canada, he fed the details of the crimes and their locations into the computer and waited for Orion to work its magic. Orion created a profile which featured one huge, red peak. It was over W4 — Chiswick, the home of Edgar Eugene Pearce at 12, Cambridge Road North.

This profile suddenly reduced a city of seven million people down to several hundred thousand. However, with an area pinpointed as the likely location of the Mardi Gra bomber, there was still a big problem. There is no database of serial bombers. Pearce's name wasn't on the other database of disgruntled Barclays customers. So knowing where he was from was not immediately helpful other than in confirming police suspicions they were dealing with a person local to west London.

But it was a start.

Bombing by Proxy

Welcome to the Mardi Gra Experience

★ ★ ★

On Saturday, November 15, 1997, Detective Chief Superintendent Jeffery Rees was the senior on-call officer for the Organised Crime Group of Scotland Yard's Specialist Operations department. A lifelong Met officer, Rees joined the force at nineteen, rising to become one of the OCG's three senior investigators. He has a reputation for being methodical and uncompromising.

At around 1.00 p.m. that day, the insistent bleep of his pager told him his afternoon at home was about to be prematurely ended. A call to the Yard's control room confirmed it. Mardi Gra had struck again . . .

Earlier that morning an odd looking video case had been found near the checkout tills of a Sainsbury's branch in Long Drive, South Ruislip. The case belonged to the film Grand Canyon and was found in an abandoned Sainsbury's carrier bag of groceries. What was odd about the case was the blue sticker stuck on it:

LOST VIDEOS

£5 REWARD!

IF YOU FIND THIS VIDEO

TAKE IT TO YOUR LOCAL

SAINSBURY VIDEO SECTION

AND CLAIM A £5 REWARD

There was, of course, no such reward scheme operating in that store or any other. Fearing the worst, security staff evacuated the supermarket and called the police. SO13 confirmed the device was the work of Mardi Gra. Pearce had dug himself out of his mental trough and returned to the tried and trusted method he first employed to deliver his bombs.

At 2.20pm that same afternoon a Grand Canyon video case exploded in the hands of a shopper who had found it in a bag left near the main entrance of the Sainsbury's store on The Broadway, West Ealing — the scene of Pearce's last attack on Barclays in April 1996. The shopper, Michael Charalambous, escaped with minor injuries. An hour-and-a-half later, there was another explosion, this time at a Sainsbury's in Greenford. The video had been handed in by a customer and went off as it was being examined in the Customer Services area.

All three bombs were versions of Pearce's original shotgun cartridge devices, designed to discharge pellets into the body or face of the person opening the case.

That evening, Rees chaired a tense meeting at the Yard. Attending were senior members of Sainsbury's security staff and officers from SO13 and the Organised Crime

Group. They discussed the nature of the attacks and the investigative work that was being done, which included reviewing hours of the supermarket's security camera footage. With three attacks in one afternoon, it was a good bet the bomber had been captured on film. But what they really had to get to grips with was just what level of threat Mardi Gra now presented.

Mardi Gra's ability to chop and change his tactics was, as ever, his greatest strength. And his style of attack on these three supermarkets had been particularly ingenious — callous, but ingenious. Using the temptation of a reward, Pearce was inducing customers to take the bombs into supermarkets for him. He was, to quote Rees, 'bombing by proxy'. This method of attack decreased Pearce's chances of being caught by enabling him to put as much space between himself and his bombs before the moment of detonation. By leaving the video case in a supermarket bag, if he was spotted walking off without the bag, it would just be thought he had forgotten his shopping. And anyone looking in the bag would see nothing other than a jumble of groceries. Pearce told the police, 'I put them down outside stores pretending to do up my shoelace and walked off. I made sure there were no video cameras around.'

In assessing Pearce's current risk status, there was bad news from the forensic explosives experts. They had discovered an alarming change in the method of construction. In his previous shotgun cartridge devices, many of the component parts had been blown apart by force of the explosion, thus lessening the force with which the pellets were expressed outwards. In particular, the 'barrels' Pearce had fashioned on the devices to give the shot more direction and force had always split, further dissipating the force of the blast. This factor had saved everyone on the receiving end of a Mardi Gra device from serious injury. However, these new video case devices were different, better built. The barrels had been strengthened with plumbing joints, robustly soldered in place to act as compression chambers to increase the velocity of the shot. In general, all aspects of the devices had been made more durable and less vulnerable to self-destruction. With devices like these, said the experts, Mardi Gra was definitely capable of killing.

This was exactly the message Pearce wanted to get across. He later confessed that during his 'period of review' between April 1996 and 1997 attacks, he had concluded that if he made his devices more dangerous it would panic Sainsbury's into paying up. He banked on forensic scientists to spot this and relay it back to the police and the company. His exact words to the police regarding this are, 'I simply wanted a business proposition. There was no value in huge explosions. A new idea was chambering the charges, which made them more lethal. If the recipient knows it can be used, then it has a point.'

With the increased media coverage caused by these more dangerous explosions, Pearce figured it would only be a matter of time before he got his way.

Putting aside his potential capability to maim or even kill, Mardi Gra's manipulation of the media was Rees's major tactical concern. He knew Pearce was feeding on the coverage and that nothing was going to stop that from happening now the whole country knew about The Mardi Gra Experience. Yet he found himself faced with a serious dilemma about how much information they should release. 'On the one hand we wanted publicity and wanted help from the public and we wanted people to be very alert, but at the same time any message from us might trigger something worse.' Rees was walking a very fine line, but faced with the coverage that was beginning to emerge, he had to give serious consideration to imposing another blackout. This coverage mainly concerned the possible identity of the bomber, and by late 1997 speculation was reaching fever pitch. With no definitive target or group with which to identify the attacks, the media found themselves in the same position as the police — looking for an invisible man.

They found dozens of different versions of him. To fill the vacuum, many papers employed the services of forensic psychologists to draw up profiles of Mardi Gra, knowing the police had done exactly the same. But with the police keeping their profile under wraps, they had to try to replicate that process based on the information which was available publicly.

Many of the psychologists drafted in by newspapers and television channels agreed with Professor Bill Tafoya's statement that Mardi Gra was looking for attention, not money. Carol Sellers, a forensic clinical psychologist, told the *Independent*, 'For most people who get involved in blackmail it's a one-off thing because they don't want to get caught. Where somebody keeps making demands this suggests a more psychological element, a concern about something that happened in the past.

'The Mardi Gra case is most unusual because of the sheer persistence of the individual concerned. Whatever happened is psychologically very important to this person.' Mardi Gra, she said, was also feeding off the publicity his campaign was generating. 'The need to be noticed is more important than any desire to hurt.' But she warned that if Mardi Gra thought causing more injuries would lead to more publicity, he might resort to 'extreme action' to achieve that.

Exactly Rees's fear.

If Mardi Gra was a person with low self-esteem, someone who sulked in the shadows of others, then the sudden experience of basking in the lime light he was enjoying could lead to nothing else but more bombs. Fire needs fuel, and Mardi Gra was being fed every day.

As the forensic consultant for the popular television series *Cracker*, which follows the work of the forensic psychologist Fitz, Ian Stephen had more requests than most for his help in profiling the bomber. He too was alarmed by how Mardi Gra seemed to be flexing his muscles.

'There is the potential to kill, but what he's enjoying just now is power,' he wrote. 'He's like a puppet master pulling the strings. He's saying: "I can do this, I can leave bombs everywhere. You can't stop me. You don't know me." ' Stephen also believed Mardi Gra's weapon of choice, the explosive device, said a lot about the perpetrator. 'It's a distance weapon, there's no proximity in it. It's like people who set fires and then watch the fire engines coming. They can watch the end product from a distance. It becomes like a sort of non-personal contact sport. But it's sneakier than the person who comes up and attacks a person and stabs them. There's that power of the creation of the bomb, the timing of it, the placing of it and the ability to watch what is happening and nobody knows it is you.'

Professor Michael Rustigan, a lecturer in criminology, penned an aggressive psychological denunciation of Mardi Gra for the *Sun*. Mardi Gra was, he stated, 'a card-carrying nerd', 'a complete flop at sex', and 'a chess player rather than a footballer.' Yet beneath these tabloid exuberances, Rustigan got pretty close to nailing Pearce and the events that had shaped his life.

Rustigan said the bomber was male, white, middle

class, bright and in his 30s or 40s. He would be living alone having been married in the past, concluding this kind of person is usually unable to form stable relationships or deep friendships. 'Although he probably went to college and is of above average intelligence, he's never achieved much in life,' he wrote. 'He's the bank clerk who always wanted to be the manager, the computer worker who wanted to run his own company. It's this frustration that leads him to focus on something to take the blame — in this case a bank. Maybe he was turned down for a loan or blames the bank for ruining his small business . . . His Blues Brothers-type calling card is very significant. This is his idea of a sense of humour. He considers himself far too intelligent to be caught by the police and is playing with them. The other reason for choosing this image could be the film Reservoir Dogs. The men in that were tough, cold murderers who nevertheless were respected. Maybe that's how he sees himself.' He concluded, 'It's his desire for fame that will eventually trip him up. Eventually his taunts to the police and letters to the newspapers will give away just that bit too much information and lead to his capture. Until this man makes that mistake he'll carry on and he won't be easy to find . . . He could be living next door or working at the next desk. You would never know.'

But the voices of the professional profilers were not the only ones to be heard. Muscling in alongside them were the pundits, columnists and other experts eager for a say.

Quiet. Obsessive. Methodical. Embittered. A loner. Friendly. Shy. Addicted to power. Playing God. Skilled. Unskilled. Thrilled by danger. Reclusive. Elusive . . .

The list went on, both contradictory and revealing. These were the words and phrases used time and again to paint a portrait of the mysterious bomber.

The *Observer* asked 'How seriously should we take him?' Dubbing his campaign as 'trolley terrorism', they speculated, 'Perhaps Mardi Gra's real target is no longer Sainsbury's, but what he sees as the deadly sin of consumerism and greed. After all, Mardi Gras is followed by Lent, a period of penitence.'

In the *Sun*, John Stalker, the former deputy chief constable of Greater Manchester, managed to bridge the gap between the media and the police and in the process, make conclusions about the bomber which, like Rustigan's, turned out to be very near the mark.

Under the headline 'Inside the mind of the Mardi Gra madman', Stalker stated, 'Mardi Gra is a man. To his neighbours he'll be a friendly loner, reserved and unremarkable. He has probably failed in business and is almost certainly an ex-Barclays customer . . . He's shrewd and cautious with a ruthless arrogance'. Shoppers were 'cannon fodder in his private war'. 'Money has ceased to be an issue and political terrorism never was. The new thrill is in creating fear, embarrassing cops and escaping arrest.'

Stalker stated the bomber was not a policeman. If he were, he reasoned, he would have gone for an early delivery of the ransom money, like Rodney Whitchelo. 'No', he said, 'Mardi Gra is not in this league'.

This last comment may have been a deliberate dig to try and provoke Pearce — exactly what Rees was trying to avoid. However, deliberate provocation is something often done by psychologists, using the opportunity presented to them by newspapers to try and draw out criminals. Ian Stephen admits he tried to do this whenever he was asked to speculate about the bomber. 'I wanted him to think I thought he was a wanker. This would make him angry. He would want to prove how smart he was and this would draw him out'. Looking at Professor Bill Tafoya's highly publicised comments, one can see the same sort of teasing statements.

'The explosive devices used by Mardi Gra are very unsophisticated and take little knowledge to make . . . if Mardi Gra had the intellectual capacity to make more complex bombs, he would have done so by now . . . Mardi Gra is not to be compared to Kaczynski.'

And we need say no more about Professor Michael Rustigan's indictments of the bomber as 'a complete flop at sex' and 'a nerd too scared of others to confront them directly.'

Some of the comments got under Pearce's skin. It was all very well revelling in the publicity. But he'd have to show them he was not to be mocked. He knew their game.

Pearce *did* show them again ten days after his re-emergence with a rapid double attack on November 25. By now, Rees had been handed command of the operation and was to be the one to bring it to its conclusion.

The first device in Chislehurst, Kent, was found by two beat bobbies. It had exploded on its own. The blackened video case was lying in the drive of an empty house around 500 yards from the local Sainsbury's store. Pearce, having seen the wide media coverage his reward stickers on the 'Grand Canyon' devices had received, assumed no-one would now fall for this trick. So he adapted it. On the front of this device, Pearce had affixed a red dot and a small sticker stating any video bearing a red dot had been 'cleared by Sainsbury's security staff'. 'That was a really deliberate attempt to get people to open these devices thinking they were safe,' says Rees.

Pearce admits this is true. 'I put a slightly different message in the last two, that is, these have been checked by security. I aimed to counteract the publicised statement that they weren't safe,' he says.

What is horrifying about this device is that the drive of the house it was left at is opposite a primary school. An abandoned video tape would be tempting to any child and the consequences of opening one of Pearce's shotgun bombs would have been devastating. He too appeared concerned by this, but his concern is couched in terms of self defence and justification. At one point he even tries to blame Sainsbury's security staff for the injuries he caused because they didn't find his devices in time.

'No-one was injured except slightly. One can never be confident of anything, but all the way through I could have created far more havoc, but I never did. I know from the TV news that there were no serious injuries . . . I didn't like to think of children taking them . . . My aim was for security staff to be on their toes and collect them. Injuries simply weren't necessary.'

Pearce seems not to want to confront the truth. He was placing bombs up to a hundred metres from some stores. How could he expect anyone to believe he genuinely thought these devices would be found by security staff?

An hour after the Chislehurst device was found, a customer at Sainsbury's Burnt Ash store in Lee Green wandered over to the Customer Services desk with an abandoned bag of shopping found just outside the store. Gingerly, the staff manning the desk looked inside the Sainsbury's carrier bag. In amongst an assortment of innocuous groceries nestled a video case bearing a red dot and a suspicious looking label. The police were called, followed hotly by SO13 who disabled the device.

The two new attacks made big news. But what really sent the media into a spin of speculative frenzy was the discovery of women's clothes near the scene of the Chislehurst device. A passer-by had found a pair of black slacks and a red woman's blouse draped over a bush in an alleyway next to the house the video was planted at. The clothes were a large size. Next to the clothes was an abandoned Sainsbury's carrier bag containing two chocolate cakes, three packets of biscuits and a packet of crisps.

It was a wonderful new twist to the story, exploited joyously by the media. From the restrained 'Mardi Gra bomber may be a woman' of the *Sunday Times* to the enthusiastic 'Bomber in woman's clothes — drag disguise may trap the mad attacker' of the *Mirror*, the possibility that the bomber was a cross-dresser added to his mystique and demonstrated better than ever his wily cunning. He was now a 'master of disguise'. As it turned out, the clothes were a total red herring and nothing to do with Pearce at all.

Perhaps the saddest episode related to the Mardi Gra case was triggered by a bomb left at a Sainsbury's store in Uxbridge Road, West Ealing on December 6. That bomb was to lead to the only death of the campaign, albeit caused indirectly.

Joan Kane was 73 years old and suffered from rheumatoid arthritis. Because of this, she made a special weekly journey from her home in Hanwell, west London to the Sainsbury's in West Ealing because it specialised in assisting the elderly with their shopping. Staff at the store did the packing and carrying and, importantly for Joan, helped her count the money her fingers had so much difficulty in handling.

At around 1.00 p.m. that day, Joan finished her shopping and made her way to the bus stop on the Uxbridge Road. She put her two bags on the floor while she waited, easing the strain on her hands. When the bus arrived she got on board, not noticing that instead of two bags, she was now carrying three. It's a 30-minute journey from the Sainsbury's store to Joan's home, involving a change of bus half way through. Joan carried her extra bag throughout the whole journey, keeping it close to her body along with the rest of her precious shopping. It was only when she got home to unpack that she realised she had gained a bag. Rummaging through it, her hand fastened on a large black lump, which she pulled from the bag. It was a Mardi Gra bomb. Unlike the previous five devices, this bomb was not encased in a video box, but was the 'improvised shotgun device' Pearce was to stick with for the rest of the campaign. By far his most deadly creation, the shotgun bomb was about 20 centimetres long. It had a short, thick single barrel which housed a primed shotgun cartridge angled upwards at 45 degrees to cause maximum damage. Not having any idea what she had in her hand, Joan fiddled with it, poking at the firing spring which was timed to release at any second. At that moment Joan's neighbour popped in to see if the old lady needed a hand. Joan turned to greet her, the bomb in her hand.

'What do you think this is Linda?' she asked innocently.

The answer was to end her life prematurely.

'Oh my God. It's a bomb. Get out!'

The bomb squad officers who attended the scene found the device still sitting on the kitchen's worktop. After disarming it, they reported the device could have got off at any time during Joan's bus trip or when she was unpacking. The whole incident proved devastating for Joan. She began to suffer flashbacks about what might have happened. Her family and neighbours would find her sitting alone in tears. She became a recluse and refused ever to go shopping alone again. The decline she sank into claimed her life. Within six weeks of the bomb find, Joan was diagnosed as having a particularly aggressive form of leukaemia. A month later, she was dead.

'Her peace of mind was destroyed,' says her daughter Maureen March. 'The doctors were in no doubt that the shock of the bomb accelerated her condition. She just ebbed away.'

Maureen firmly believes Pearce was responsible for her mother's death. Shortly after Joan died, she wrote an angry open letter to the Mardi Gra bomber in her local newspaper. 'If the person who left the bomb has any feelings, he will realise he might just as well have blown her up when she took the bomb home because the outcome was the same.'

After the attack on December 6th, the police were anticipating a Christmas campaign designed to wreck Sainsbury's trade. They cast around to try and find any clue from the trail of debris that might lead them to the bomber's door. The bomber's use of Sainsbury's carrier bags gave the police an idea. Every carrier bag has a tiny colour coded batch number near its base. The code is so small hardly anyone knows it's there. It was a virtual certainty that Mardi Gra was a Sainsbury's shopper himself and would therefore probably do all his shopping at his local store. If they could identify the store from the bags he used to conceal his bombs, it would suddenly give them a very narrow focus on which to concentrate their resources. Rees ordered the bags examined. The results were a complete surprise. 'I couldn't believe it,' says Rees. 'Every number on every bag Mardi Gra used had been carefully and neatly razored out. None of us had even noticed there were numbers on the bags and yet here we were faced with someone who had thought of every detail and every possible flaw in his plan. It was a sign to us that we were dealing with someone who was really taking us on.'

Pearce had another surprise in store for the police and Sainsbury's. He did nothing. As he had the year before, Pearce decided for whatever reason to keep his unseasonal cheer to himself.

A few days before Christmas, the Mardi Gra team made a decision to pay the bomber. The failed attempts to negotiate had taught them that Mardi Gra would not communicate on any terms other than his own. In his last letter, sent that month to Sainsbury's, he had demanded £10,000 per day, without limit of time. He wanted promotional plastic cards manufactured and given away with *Exchange & Mart*. These cards would appear to be promoting the new Sainsbury's Internet site. As with his Barclays plan, they would have an active magnetic strip on the back which had been coded with a PIN number known only by Pearce, enabling him to use them as cash cards. On December 27, a brief message appeared in the *Daily Telegraph* personals:

M. Work will be completed and ready for London circulation on Thursday 26th March 1998. This is the earliest possible date. Hope it meets your schedule. G

The Met had to hope this would work. If he wouldn't communicate, the only way to get Mardi Gra would be to catch him red-handed. But would he come out for the bait?

Pearce replied to the advert on January 16, 1998 by placing a bomb in his own branch of Sainsbury's in Essex Place, just off Chiswick High Road. The store is a five-minute walk from Pearce's home. It was the place he always shopped because despite his predilection for bombing and blackmail, Pearce was a loyal and regular customer. The

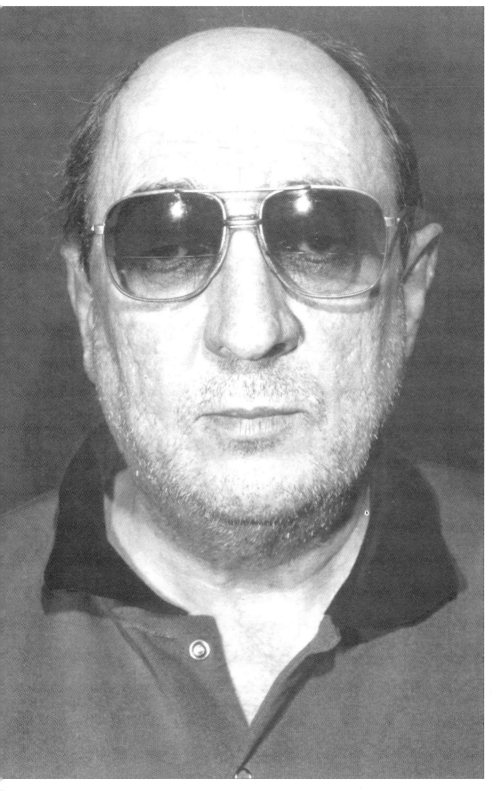

Edgar Pearce, photographed shortly after his arrest with his brother, Russell, in Whitton High Street.

Above: One of the first six packages sent by Mardi Gra.

Right: A typical Mardi Gra device: crude, but very effective.

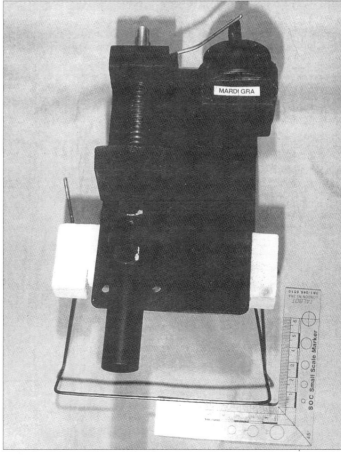

The leafy Chiswick council home of Edgar Pearce.

Top left and right: The tumbledown green house where Edgar made his bombs.

Bottom: Whitton High Street, scene of two Mardi Gra bombs, and the Pearce brothers' arrests.

Top: Edgar's local, which he bombed during the media blackout to check that his devices were getting through.

Bottom: Edgar caught in the act. He can be seen crossing the road in front of the bus, carrying his bomb.

CASHLINE TRAP
and video spies catch Mardi Gra bomb suspects

WHERE THE BOMBERS STRUCK

1	Hampstead, North London	Dec 6 1994
2	Ladbroke Grove, West London	Dec 6 1994
3	Hammersmith, West London	Dec 6 1994
4	Earls Court, West London	Dec 6 1994
5	Kensington, West London	Dec 6 1994
6	Paddington, West London	Dec 6 1994
7	Cambridge	May 19 1995
8	Chiswick, West London	Jun 5 1995
9	Dymchurch, Kent	Jun 10 1995
10	Northampton, Northants	Jun 22 1995
11	Berkhamstead, Herts	Jul 5 1995
12	Amersham, Bucks	Jul 14 1995
13	Richmond, Surrey	Jul 18 1995
14	Welling, Kent	Aug 29 1995
15	Walton, Middx	Sept 12 1995
16	Walton, Middx	Sept 13 1995
17	Woolwich, South East London	Sept 27 1995
18	Southall, Middx	Oct 7 1995
19	Welling, Kent	Oct 24 1995
20	Eltham, South East London	Nov 30 1995
21	Southall, Middx	Dec 12 1995
22	Acton, West London	Jan 6 1996
23	Ealing, West London	Jan 30 1996
24	Eltham, South East London	Feb 5 1996
25	Ealing, West London	Apr 20 1996
26	Marylebone, central London	Sept 2 1997
27	Ruislip, Middlesex	Nov 15 1997
28	Ealing, West London	Nov 15 1997
29	Greenford, Middx	Nov 15 1997
30	Chiselhurst, Kent	Nov 15 1997
31	Lee Green, South East London	Nov 30 1997
32	Forest Hill, South East London	Feb 12 1998
33	Forest Hill, South East London	Mar 4 1998
34	Eltham, South East London	Mar 17 1998

BOMB THREATS
Letter sent to head of security at Barclaycard — Aug 2 1995
Head of security at Sainsbury's HQ London — Jul 11 1996

TERROR IN NEATLY WRAPPED PARCELS

By JEFF EDWARDS

THE Mardi Gra bombings began in December 1994 when six devices arrived in the post at Barclays Bank branches in west London.

They were inside video boxes, wrapped neatly in Christmas paper and here stickers reading: Welcome to the Mardi Gra experience.

A woman employee was slightly injured when she opened a box, triggering a home-made device that detonated a shotgun cartridge.

In May, June and July, six more bombs were sent by mail to private individuals or small businesses.

They included a tax inspector in Cambridgeshire, a camera shop in Chiswick, and a publican in Chiswick, west ...

communication and started a fresh wave of bombs. Between late 1995 and early 1996, 12 more were either posted or ...

SEARCH: Police examine a Sainsbury's bag in Pearce's garden · Pictures: JASON SHILLINGFORD

branch of the Metropolitan police and the newly-formed National Crime Squad.

The secret account was linked to an ultra-sophisticated computer that would trigger an alarm at the Yard within three seconds of Mardi Gra tapping in his PIN number.

And on Tuesday afternoon, the trap was sprung. Last week a similar alert had come from a Barclays branch in Ealing, west London, after money was withdrawn from a cashpoint.

That time watching police were unable to catch the suspects. Yesterday, £250 withdrawn from the Barclays branch in £20 and £10 notes was seized at Edgar Pearce's home.

The raid was authorised after a top-level Yard conference involving the Deputy Assistant Commissioner, the Organised Crime Group, the Anti-Terrorist Squad, and Det Supt Jeff Rees, in charge of Operation Heath.

In the early hours, armed police broke down the door of Edgar Pearce's home in a quiet tree-lined avenue.

Apart from home-made bombs, they found two pistols, rounds of 762 army-issue rifle ammunition, 12-bore and .410 shotgun cartridges, springs and nails, and video boxes.

Disguises, including wigs and false beards, were also discovered.

Tools found included power drills, hacksaws, metal files, adhesives and

electric soldering irons. An SLR camera with a selection of lenses, plus dozens of items of clothing, were taken away for forensic examination.

Police scientists began an inch by inch examination of the house.

Asleep

They also studied a video surveillance camera covering the front door, which was installed about a year ago.

Two men asleep at the house were held, but found to be tenants of Edgar Pearce.

More bomb equipment was uncovered in a rented lock-up garage in a near... later put... section garden.

At the small one Neigh... said: "I greenho morning...

"We all and just be by le...

These l lives at by his Pearce flat b... "I can...

A selection of the amazing press coverage received after the police went public. The case was almost unprecedented in its cunning and ambition, and the media were fascinated by it.

How long befor... macabre gam...

He is behind 30 bomb attacks an... detectives believ... he is Britain's most dangerous psychopath. Wha... is going on in his demented mind?

by James Dalrymple

AT THIS precise moment he is almost certainly hard at work. A quiet man in a quiet room, tinkering lovingly with strange little mechanisms and planning his next move. Christmas is coming and he seems to have his best work for the festive season.

He may be in a locked room of his house. The man's money says he will live on his own. Or, if he has a wife and family, he may spend a lot of time in a padlocked shed.

We know only two things about him. That he probably lives somewhere in the south of England, given his targets, and that he is in one of his active phases. He is also starting to enjoy himself, even leaving strange clues such as an imported cream cake scattered around.

And he can read about his exploits in the papers, after all, he has the two things essential to all celebrities: an instantly recognisable name and public attention.

The Mardi Gra Bomber is in no hurry. It has been just over a week since we last heard from him. And a large force of dedicated police officers can only wait to see what his next move will be.

So who is this person who has left 38 intricate bombs, often containing shotgun cartridges and rifle bullets that explode out of books, magazines and video boxes, across London and the south of England?

The detectives have few clues, beyond that his targets include Barclays and Sainsbury's. Experts who have examined the cleverly made bombs estimate that each one can take up to seven days to construct. And over the years he has demonstrated his patience. He has sometimes remained dormant for months. At other times he erupts in a frenzy.

His pleasure, it seems, is concerned mainly in the construction of his lethal toys and the planning of their delivery. That is what the game is all about.

TO THE elite squad of hand-picked detectives from Scotland Yard's Organised Crime Group, backed by a group of criminal psychologists who have been tracking him for years, he remains a total mystery.

You can imagine him at work. They see him bent over his bench, using a large magnifying glass, surrounded by odds-and-ends rank of tools.

He will be using tiny soldering irons, electric drills and saws, alongside tubes of insulation tape.

He will choose from a variety of shotgun cartridges and metal-jacketed bullets, probably bought in great secrecy on trips abroad, and butane gas containers normally used to fill lighters.

And for the fine work he will have rolls of thin steel wire, miniature spring clips, boxes of tiny screws and thin metal tubes ground and polished to pin-barrel condition.

In another part of the room he will have an expensive computer, with desktop publishing software and a photo-scanner.

He likes to stick copies of the logos of British Airways, United Colours of Benetton and the Halifax Building Society onto the packages containing his devices. It gives them a cheerful official look. On a shelf nearby will be rows of videos. One he particularly liked was an American drama called Grand Canyon.

first three letters of the title — Gra — informed the police that the Mardi Gra Bomber was back in business after an absence of 11 months.

On November 18, as part of his latest series of attacks, he planted a Grand Canyon cassette — containing a 12-bore shotgun cartridge wired to a spring-loaded trigger — in a bag of groceries at a branch of Sainsbury's in Ruislip.

It had a label telling the finder to take it to the store's video department to claim a £5 reward. There was even a little note saying the cassette had been checked by security staff, such is his attention to detail.

It was the 36th device sent by the Mardi Gra bomber since he began his bombing spree in December 1994. It was one of five similar devices delivered both by post and in person to Sainsbury's branches in Ruislip, Ealing, Greenford, Chislehurst, and Catford.

ALTHOUGH three of them exploded, thankfully causing no injuries, the others were designed not to go off. This is just one of the many paradoxes that have mystified police. By leaving out one vital component, the bomber deliberately renders many of his devices harmless. This is all part of his game.

"He is telling us that he decides when a device can kill," says a police source. "What he is saying is 'This time I have left out a bit of the equipment. But the next time I will complete it.'"

"This is one of the most ... dangerous men we have ever dealt with, and we are convinced that some day he will raise the stakes and produce bombs capable of killing large numbers of people. This is the nature of such freaks."

Criminal psychologist Professor David Canter of Liverpool University says the bomber is on an escalating course that could lead to murder.

"There are a great number of reasons for what he is doing and it has become a way of life for him," he says. "It is all about the thrill of the chase and getting intense excitement from fooling the police.

"It was probably sparked off by revenge for some small insult. But in his mind he is some kind of hero. The planning of his campaign has become the driving force of his life."

The Mardi Gra bomber's campaign can be split into three phases. The first reason behind it could be linked to Canter's theory of a 'small insult'.

The police are convinced the insult could have come from dealings with Barclays.

His frenzied opening salvo was targeted at the bank in December 1994, when he sent six devices through the post on the same day to six branches in West and North London.

Identically wrapped in Christmas paper, the video cases had cover photographs showing a group of men in dark suits and dark glasses, and bearing the cheerful message: 'Welcome to the Mardi Gra experience.'

The cassettes held a single shotgun cartridge, primed by a spring-loaded mounting and designed to fire when opened. Two exploded, one injuring a

EX-POLICE CHIEF JOHN STALKER INVESTIGATES

Inside the mind of Mardi Gra madman

THE Mardi Gra bomber carried out his 35th attack yesterday. Police now fear it is only a matter of time before he kills.

The explosion in Forest Hill, south London, is the latest in a four-year campaign of terror against Barclays Bank and Sainsbury's around London and the Home Counties. The fiend sends blackmail notes demanding millions, but so far has not received a penny.

Despite a massive hunt, there are few clues to his identity. Here John Stalker — former Deputy Chief Constable of Greater Manchester Police — carries out his own investigation for The Sun, starting with a profile of the madman.

THE PROFILE

I BELIEVE that Mardi Gra is a man. Women plant bombs but they do not make them.

Time after time he has avoided security cameras and police stake-outs.

Once, after planting a murderous device, he discarded women's clothing. It was probably a bluff but if not he could be an experienced cross-dresser comfortable in public in women's clothing.

Assembling the bombs is the work of a man with practised hands. He is shrewd and cautious with a ruthless arrogance.

He sees the police as individually stupid but is careful of their routines and resources.

His real enemies are not the cops but Barclays Bank and Sainsbury's, and those who do business with them.

He is contemptuous towards innocent shoppers who might be maimed or killed. They are cannon fodder in his private war with adversaries who he believes have hurt or humiliated him.

Thrill

His blackmail attempts have so far failed. Not a penny has been paid and my belief is he does not much care now.

Money has ceased to be the issue and political terrorism never was.

The new thrill is in creating fear, embarrassing the cops and escaping arrest.

To his neighbours he will be a friendly loner, reserved and unremarkable. He has probably failed in business and is almost certainly an ex-Barclays customer.

He lives or lived in west London and is single or separated. He might drive an older, beautifully-kept car.

Speculation last week that Mardi Gra is a cop will prove to be wide of the mark, although his bomb-making knowledge suggests he may, years ago, have been associated with the police or Army.

I do not think he has ever been in prison. A seriously bent policeman, such as detective Rodney Whitchelo, jailed in 1990 for 17 years for supermarket blackmail, would focus much more on the early delivery of ransom cash. Mardi Gra is not in this league.

For 18 months, from April 96 to November 97, the bombings stopped. My guess is that Mardi Gra was in a relationship he could not sustain.

When it ended, it was bombing business as usual - but with added hatred.

CHILLING .. Mardi Gra calling card sent with parcel bombs to Barclays branches in 1994

BLAST .. remains of incendiary device

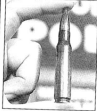

DEMAND .. blackmailer sent bullet to store

THE CLUES

THE bomber is cold, calculating and clever. So far he has been smart enough not to leave many clues.

Although crudely designed, his bombs are carefully crafted from copper tubing and shotgun cartridge explosive hidden in video cassettes or plastic shopping bags.

Some failed to detonate but remained extremely dangerous.

Obviously, he is learning from earlier technical mistakes.

He has been meticulous in avoiding detection. His mocking extortion letters are written on a standard word processor.

Only the bomber knows why he chose the name

Shrove Tuesday. In a letter last year he used the name MARDIne GRAham but he was playing mind games with the police.

He also claims Mardi Gra is an angry group of Barclays Bank "victims".

This is no empty boast. Mardi Gra almost certainly operates alone.

Obvious clues lie in his choice of targets. The first 25 bombs were aimed at branches or customers of Barclays Bank or Barclaycard.

As bank security improved — and for no solid reasons he has explained — Sainsbury's became the new object of his bitter hatred.

The pattern of attacks — all but two in the London area — has given us no clues.

TIMETABLE OF TERROR
HERE is the Mardi Gra bomber's catalogue of terror:
1 December 6, 1994: Barclays Bank, Hampstead, London.
2 December 6, 1994: Barclays, Ladbroke Grove, London.
3 December 6, 1994: Barclays, Hammersmith.
4 December 6, 1994: Barclays, Earls Court.
5 December 6, 1994: Barclays, Kensington.
6 December 6, 1994: Barclays, Paddington.
7 May 19, 1995: Private address in Cambridge.
8 June 9, 1995: Pub in Chiswick, London.
9 June 10, 1995: Camera shop in Dymchurch, Kent.
10 June 20, 1995: Barclaycard HQ, Northampton.
11 July 5, 1995: Barclays, Bexhamsted, Herts.
12 July 14, 1995: Private address in Amersham, Bucks.
13 July 15, 1995: Private address in Richmond, Surrey.
14 August 10, 1995: Private address in Welling, Kent.
15 September 12, 1995: Office in Whitley, Bucks.
16 September 12, 1995: Another office in Whitley, Bucks.
17 September 27, 1995: Office in Woolwich, London.
18 October 2, 1995: Rymans in Chiswick, London.
19 October 28, 1995: Telephone box in Welling, Kent.
20 November 20, 1995: Telephone box in Eltham.
21 December 12, 1995: Private address in Southall, Middx.
22 December 15, 1995: Telephone box in Acton, London.
23 January 30, 1996: Barclays Bank, Ealing.
24 February 5, 1996: Barclays Bank, Eltham, London.
25 April 20, 1996: Barclays Bank, Ealing London.
26 November 15, 1997: Sainsbury's, Ruislip, Middx.
27 November 15, 1997: Sainsbury's, Forest Hill, London.
28 November 18, 1997: Sainsbury's, Greenford, Middx.
29 November 18, 1997: Sainsbury's, Chalmfard, Kent.
30 November 18, 1997: Sainsbury's, Clifford, London.
31 December 6, 1997: Sainsbury's, Ealing, London.
32 January 16, 1998: Sainsbury's, Chiswick.
33 February 5, 1998: Sainsbury's, Ealing.
34 February 12, 1998: Sainsbury's, Forest Hill, London.
35 March 5, 1998: Sainsbury's, Forest Hill, London.

THE POLICE INVESTIGATION

THE hunt is a detective's nightmare. Mardi Gra is a grey face operating intermittently in a city of seven million people.

For the first 16 months, hoping to trap him, Scotland Yard and Barclays kept the investigation under wraps without seeking the help of the public.

It was a tricky decision which may have backfired. In that time Mardi Gra planted 25 bombs and polished his deadly skills.

The investigation to catch him is massive, with Anti-Terrorist and Crime Squad officers assisted by MI5, criminal psychologists and bank security agents.

My fear is that the challenge is growing stale and he will up the stakes and begin bombing outside London or find new targets.

The whole of Britain could be his battleground. After 35 successes he believes he is untouchable and the risk of deaths increases by the day.

Mardi Gra is beginning a new bombing spree. Behaviour patterns point to an imminent blitz of five or more bombs in one day.

Curiously, last week Scotland Yard Commissioner Sir Paul Condon purposely imposed another Mardi Gra information blackout.

There will be operational reasons for this decision I have made similar ones myself in the deadly game of cat and mouse between police and bomber. But shutting out the public is a high risk strategy. Clever and persistent terrorists are usually caught with public help.

Mardi Gra's reign of terror has gone on for over three years without much public awareness and

SHOP BOMB F

Trolley terrorism. By Mark Honigsbaum

The cake-box bomber

He hides explosives in chocolate sponges. How seriously should we take him?

THE CALLING CARD
One of the six firebombs posted to different branches of Barclays Bank.

THE BULLET IN THE POST
Sent by Mardi Gra to Sainsbury's with a threatening letter.

THE TEA-TIME SURPRISE
Detective Superintendent Jeffrey Rees with a cake box left near a home.

THE SCENE OF THE CRIME
This Sainsbury's in Forest Hill, site of two bombs.

CHOCOLATE & ORANGE CAKE

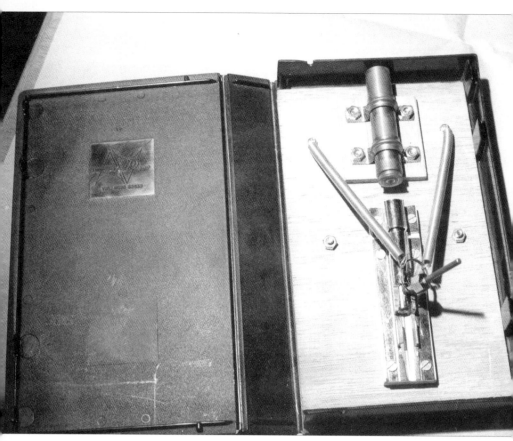

Above: A police replica of a video case booby-trap bomb, similar to the ones made by Edgar Pearce.

Personal

AUTHORS: Manuscripts wanted by publisher for U.K./U.S.A. Call Dorrance Publishing

IDEAS/INVENTIONS Wanted by large Intl.Co. Call ISO FREE on

MARDI GRA
We are ready to help and give value. Contact us on the verification number

Above: A personal ad placed by the police to Mardi Gra.

Right: The sticker that Pearce placed on video boxes.

LOST VIDEOS
£5 REWARD!
IF YOU FIND THIS VIDEO TAKE IT TO YOUR LOCAL SAINSBURY VIDEO SECTION AND CLAIM A £5 REWARD

cupboards of Cambridge Road North, now locked up and empty, still bear witness to this. They contain the sad remnants of his larder — Sainsbury's own brand Chilli Con Carne, Sainsbury's own brand Apple Sauce and Sainsbury's own brand Olive Oil. And upon hearing his arrest one of the few things his dazed daughter Nicola could say was, 'My dad shops at Sainsbury's because he likes their food. He doesn't go there to bomb them.'

Pearce was blind drunk the day he attacked his own Sainsbury's. After doing his normal shopping, he left his 'thank you' gift four yards outside the main entrance. At 18.45 the bag was discovered and the area sealed off. Pearce didn't go straight home after planting the bomb. It's believed he went straight to see his brother, Ronald.

When Edgar did eventually stagger home, one of his lodgers was in the kitchen, cursing the disruption caused by the bomb which had prevented him from getting home on time. The lodger told his landlord about the bomb. Pearce's only response was to slur, 'That fucking Mardi Gra bomber!' before bursting into laughter. There was admiration in his tone. He was feeling very pleased with himself. The supermarket was going to pay. He was going to get his money.

'That fucking Mardi Gra bomber!' Pearce saw himself as some latter-day Scarlet Pimpernel; elusive, cunning, daring. It was a vision which was a lot better than the actual reflection he saw in the mirror — a fat ageing drunk with no prospects and only a council rent book and an old car to his name.

Pearce continued to bomb, with two attacks in a one-week period during the beginning of February. The first was left at the same bus stop as Joan Kane's bomb. This time, however, the bomb detonated before anyone had a chance to pick it up. Witnesses told how shrapnel was sent flying in all directions across the street. There were only about fifteen people in the area when the device went off and no-one was injured.

Seven days later in Forest Hill, south east London, factory worker Ian Clark stopped off at a cashpoint machine which stood 100 metres from the local Sainsbury's store. It was just gone five in the morning and Ian was on his way to work in Northfleet, Kent. Sitting by the side of the machine was a bag full of groceries. Not one to look a gift horse in the mouth, Ian picked the bag up and placed it on the passenger seat of his car and drove off. Twenty minutes later the bag exploded as Ian drove down the A2, filling the car with smoke and flying debris. Ian was saved from serious injury by the fact the bomb had tipped over inside the bag, so that the barrel was facing down into the seat. When it detonated, the force of the blast went through the floor of the car. Ian escaped with nothing worse than a few cuts and shock. After the explosion he grabbed the shredded, smoking carrier bag and threw it from the car before driving to Dartford police station. His report resulted in a nine-mile stretch of the A2 being closed in both directions while a thorough search was made for the remains of the bomb. It was Mardi Gra's 34th attack.

With Mardi Gra ignoring the offer to pay, Rees decided it was time to take the fight to him. If Mardi Gra wasn't going to respond to this offer, then the only chance the Met had was to catch him actually planting a bomb. But how?

Operation Heath didn't have much to go on, but what they had they intended to make the best use of. Detective Inspector Kim Rossmo was recalled from Canada to perform a fresh geographical profile, this time incorporating the Sainsbury's attacks. While that was being prepared, they had the old profile to go on, with its clear hotspot in the W4 area of London and a secondary hotspot in south east London. Rees admits this spread of activity confused the investigating team. 'There aren't many people who have connections in west and south east London,' he says, 'and of course we weren't to know they were the places he lived and the place his wife lived. That was the link, but from our point of view a really difficult one to find, one that was only revealed on arrest.'

Nevertheless, these two hotspots — odd and confusing as they were - were the best thing they had. It was decided to saturate these areas with covert video surveillance. Every branch of Sainsbury's in these two areas was to be covered if possible. But even with these remote, sleepless eyes watching over the potential targets, Rees still knew that Mardi Gra had the upper hand because he wasn't putting the bombs devices down at the stores themselves, but in the vicinity — maybe fifty or a hundred yards away. And with hundreds of people walking around, all with the same bags, they were going to need a bit of luck.

March 4, 1998. Seventeen-year-old Curtis Dennis was a keen and promising athlete. A college student, he also worked part-time at the Forest Hill branch of Sainsbury's. At 5.45 p.m. he was outside the store when a black plastic bin bag exploded sending pellets and shrapnel ripping into the back of his legs. Curtis was rushed to hospital for treatment to his wounds. He would require surgery and skin grafts to repair the damage. In a shop doorway, detectives found the remains of the Mardi Gra bomb. It was his standard shotgun-type device, detonated by clockwork timer. However, this one was more robust. Recent devices of this nature, such as the one taken home by poor Joan Kane, had been propped up on wire legs at an angle of 45 degrees. Pearce had obviously found this method of aiming unsatisfactory and for this attack had modified the firing platform still further by ditching the wire legs in favour of a shaped concrete block which he had manufactured in a home-made mould. The devices were mounted onto this mould with metal bolts so they had a stable platform to fire on and to ensure the direction was always at 45 degrees upwards for maximum damage potential.

'I regret the injury caused at Forest Hill,' Pearce said later. 'Although I had aimed to avoid it. I placed the device to fire across the front of the shop window fairly safely. As I was placing it in the doorway, a guy with a loud voice asked me a question and he got hold of my arm. He wouldn't let go and I ended up pushing the bag at him so he ended up holding it. I then turned and walked off. I didn't even put it down. He was probably Polish, about 60 years old, casual dressed. I didn't understand what he was saying.'

Pearce then goes on to explain why this device, unlike his others, is not in a Sainsbury's carrier bag. 'I stopped using them because they were being stolen. When I dropped them, they didn't reach the correct destination . . . later devices are in black bags from stores.'

As throughout his interviews, he attempts to make light of the danger to the public. 'I'm not leaving them pointed at people. I wanted to stop it turning over and shooting in the wrong direction. It was a black bin liner. I had dumped it to look like rubbish and it was less likely to be picked up . . . I always took great care not to hurt people.'

Eltham High Street, March 17, 1998.

'That camera finally got him there.' Jeff Rees couldn't

contain his satisfaction.

At last, the police's luck changed. For the first time they got to take a peek at their malicious adversary who had slipped by them for nearly three-and-a-half years.

At 11.59 a.m., one of the Met's covert surveillance cameras captured Mardi Gra at work as he planted one of his shotgun bombs a few yards away from the front entrance of the local Sainsbury's store. Five minutes later, the remote camera also captured the impact of the bomb as it exploded. But because it was a remote camera, by the time the footage was reviewed at the Yard, Pearce was long gone.

Jeff Rees sat down in front of the television with eager anticipation. Was this going to be the break they had waited so long for? The video started to play. Rees says, 'When I saw that video I went cold. Because although we had known there was a real threat to the public, when you actually see how fortunate we were that no-one was killed with this device, it brings it home to you exactly what you are dealing with.'

The grainy black and white footage showed Pearce striding purposefully across Eltham High Street at 11.59 a.m. Wearing a striped anorak and flat cap, he was carrying a large black bin bag in his gloved right hand. His left hand was ungloved. Without hesitation, he dumped the bag against the wall of the Sainsbury's store and twisted it so the barrel of the device hidden inside was pointing towards a bus stop where an elderly lady was standing, too engrossed in hunting through her handbag for her bus pass to notice what was going on behind her.

Pearce then turned swiftly and walked off to the left, leaving his bomb pointing straight at the oblivious pensioner. It had taken him just nine seconds to plant the bomb and disappear.

Four minutes tick by on the time-coded clock etched onto the footage. A mother and her baby in a pram stroll in front of the bag. People getting off a bus walk through the device's firing path. Thankfully, the elderly lady gets on a bus, never knowing how close she came to serious injury or possibly even death from the hidden barrel which was pointing directly towards her. The clock ticks round to 12.04. Just four seconds before the device detonates, a woman walks in front of the bag. The explosion tears the bag open, spewing shot into the bus stop. People standing nearby instinctively duck and recoil away from the noise of the explosion. Others just stare at the bag, unable to comprehend what has just happened.

Amazingly, the video was no good for an identification. Rees couldn't believe it. Just how much luck could Mardi Gra enjoy? And how much bad luck was the Met to be forced to endure? The video footage was explosive evidence in every sense of the word, but it had one major flaw. It didn't show Pearce's face. Despite having missed the camera when he had reconnoitred the street earlier that morning, Pearce never once turned in the camera's direction. He didn't even look left or right when he crossed the street, despite the fact he walked right in front of a bus. 'I mean,' exclaims Rees, 'who else crosses a road without looking left or right? All we had was a shot of him from behind. He just goes straight across, puts it down, doesn't look left or right goes straight on. So all we had was that shot. It was desperately frustrating. We couldn't even see his build. We could only estimate that it was someone aged between 35 and 65, which doesn't exactly narrow it down. But at least we knew at that stage we were dealing with a man.'

Rees now had another dilemma. Should he release the video to the media? Because the danger was high, there was a strong argument for going public just in case someone would recognise him. Bravely, Rees blocked the move, arguing that the footage wasn't good enough to identify the bomber and could actively damage the investigation. On seeing the footage Mardi Gra would immediately discard the clothes he was wearing at that time, or maybe go quiet for 12 months but then come back in an even more dangerous way. It was a decision that caused a lot of soul-searching. If another device went off soon, Rees could have a lot of explaining to do.

As it turned out, Rees was right to withhold the tape. The clothing Pearce was wearing that day was what he always wore on his bombing sprees and never at any other time. He referred to his anorak as his 'bombing jacket' and, although quite distinctive, it was one no members of his family, or indeed anyone who knew him, had ever seen because Pearce knew if he was caught on camera, no-one would recognise the anorak as being his. The same went for the flat cap.

Rees ordered a new message to be placed in the *Daily Telegraph*. 'Although we had agreed to pay, he carried on putting devices down. He really kept the pressure on us, but also gave us the moral high ground in some ways, because we were able to send a message out saying "We're playing our part, why aren't you?" When he got that one, he was convinced that this was a genuine offer to pay and that's when he stopped. And that was the important thing.'

The bomb of March 17 was to be Pearce's last.

Unmasked

Welcome to the Mardi Gra Experience

By the time of Mardi Gra's last attack, reports were beginning to surface in the media about how much the police had spent on what was so far, a totally unsuccessful investigation. Figures upwards of £1 million were widely quoted. Other estimates — up to £5 million — referred to the total cost of the campaign, incorporating the financial impact of the extra security employed by Mardi Gra's targets and their accumulated loss of business. The police have refused to release the true figure but it is believed that the total investigation costs from start to finish were £10 million, including the extra security employed by the targets, but excluding their individual business losses.

Costs, however, were the furthest thing from Jeff Rees's mind in late March of 1998. Catching Mardi Gra on tape — face or no face — was the best breakthrough the investigation had enjoyed to date. It also showed that the covert surveillance was working. Rees was keen to capitalise on the perceived advantage gained by the video footage. If they could catch Mardi Gra on camera, they could catch him in person. And maybe if Kim Rossmo's updated geographical profile could throw up new information, they could begin to narrow the borders of the investigation even further and start to corral Mardi Gra towards capture.

This optimism was to be proved to be justified. Favour was turning in the Met's direction, if only because the green light had been given for what was to turn out to be the largest covert surveillance operation ever mounted on British soil. Mardi Gra's campaign had by early 1998 touched the highest levels of government. The Home Office was becoming increasingly anxious about Mardi Gra's campaign. Sources interviewed for this book have stated that Jack Straw, the Home Secretary, told the Met's commissioner Sir Paul Condon that the capture of Mardi Gra must be of the highest priority. No government wants a mad bomber on the loose. It makes all their policy statements about being tough on crime look rather hollow if their biggest police force can't catch one man. The Met were told to get Mardi Gra — no matter what the cost.

Mardi Gra's new willingness to co-operate, combined with the determined push being given by and to the Met, steered the investigation into a new and conclusive phase. Operation Heath was entering its final stage.

It had become obvious that only by swamping Mardi Gra's hunting grounds could the police hope to come near to the bomber. But given the huge area this would cover, the manpower requirements were prohibitive. At least a thousand men would be needed to monitor all the cashpoints within Mardi Gra's area of operation.

It didn't matter. The go ahead was given for a massive, intensive, all or nothing strategy.

Hundreds of specialist surveillance officers were deployed throughout west London, particularly in W4, the Chiswick/Ealing area identified by the geographic profile. They had an almost immediate success — but not the one they expected. Officers seconded from the Flying Squad were monitoring the car park of the Sainsbury's branch in Chiswick — Pearce's local supermarket — when they saw two men 'acting suspiciously'. The men were fiddling with boxes they were loading into a car. The officers were given the go ahead to pounce. When they did, they got a good result; £1 million worth of cannabis resin, packed into the boxes they thought contained bombs.

April 1. All Fool's Day was nearing its close when Rees received the telephone call. A man had been arrested after being chased from the grounds of a Sainsbury's store in South Ruislip. A weapon had been recovered. It looked like they had Mardi Gra.

Undercover officers staking out the store were alerted that a man had been seen lurking in the vicinity of the store and nearby tube station. The man was located just as he drove off from the scene. The detectives were quickly behind him and began tailing the suspect. Meanwhile, another team of officers, some of them armed, were searching the area around the store. An unusual box was found near to where the man had last been seen and police immediately began to evacuate the store, neighbouring offices and houses closest to the suspect package. As soon as the officers following the man heard about the discovery of the box, they forced the suspect's car to a halt. After hauling the man from the driver's seat, they found a gun hidden in the car. Back in South Ruislip, SO13 carried out a controlled explosion on the box. But when they went to study the remains of the box, they discovered not bomb parts — but rat poison.

The 'Mardi Gra Bomber' turned out to be a 67-year-old part-time rat catcher. After a day of questioning to check out his story and alibis, he was charged with unlawful possession of a firearm and released.

Mardi Gra was still out there and getting ready to collect his ill-gotten gains.

'People have questioned why it took so long to catch Mardi Gra,' comments Rees. 'Well, the easy part for a blackmailer is carrying out the threat. The hard part is collecting the money.' The easy part had dragged out over three long years. Pearce was feeling secure and buoyant, unaware of the scale of events unfolding around him. And with three years having gone by, the Met were prepared to wait just that little bit longer to get their man.

A special bank account was opened and £20,000 deposited to feed Mardi Gra while the hunt for him was on. A new advert was placed in the *Telegraph* personals confirming the final arrangements.

M. Everything on schedule. Arrangements commence 8am 23.4.98. We agree on new notified number. No change possible. Thank you. The number remains in place until 8am 30.4.98 for joining. Then only the daily allowance for each of the ten items remains. This allowance is unchangeable because of the system. Any difficulties do not hesitate to write. May be in touch before 23.4.98. G.

Rees had to pray this seven-day window would be enough. On April 23, a new edition of *Exchange & Mart* went on the shelves. The magazine contained the 'promotional' Sainsbury's cards, Pearce's key to a secret fortune. The waiting game started.

The Operation Heath team had no fixed target to aim for, and were faced with the logistical headache of having to set up hundreds of Observation Posts (OPs). With west London already identified as Mardi Gra's hunting ground, every cash point in the area was surveyed for its suitability. At the same time, all CCTV cameras, police surveillance cameras and bank and building society cameras were checked to ensure they were fully working and looking in the right place.

The surveillance teams were organised in clusters covering the most likely spots. The 1,000-strong police team which lay in wait for Pearce included 250 surveillance specialists from the National Crime Squad which been set up in April 1998 mainly to combat organised crime. It's been called the English equivalent of the FBI — a force which can operate across the boundaries of the regional constabularies.

In addition to the overwhelming manpower that was deployed, the Met also turned to computer technology to help them snare Mardi Gra. The cashpoint computers were programmed to alert a computer in the New Scotland Yard control room as soon as the blackmailer entered the secret PIN number. However, having this electronic alert did not mean the Mardi Gra was sure to be arrested as soon as he withdrew money. Because in recent years, nearly every cashpoint network has joined a nationwide link to allow customers greater access. Barclays customers can use Nationwide machines; Nat West customers can use Lloyds machines; most machines will let you draw money out if you have a VISA card. For the blackmailer, it means he has carte blanche to use virtually any machine in the country. So if Pearce decided to take money out in say, Kent, there would be no-one on the ground to stop him. And even if he stayed in London, there are so many machines and London traffic is so notoriously bad, that getting the nearest surveillance team to the target in time could be a tall order. A cash withdrawal takes about 40 seconds, so in reality, unless a surveillance team was actually at a cashpoint when Mardi Gra was there, the chances of getting to him were slim.

But the police had one more trick available to them. The cashpoint computers were programmed to delay payment on a progressively increasing scale, so that every time Mardi Gra entered the PIN, the computer would take a few seconds longer than it did the last time to process the transaction. By building in their ever-increasing delay, if Mardi Gra was making several withdrawals at a time in one area, the police could quickly flood that area to cover every machine. Once that happened, in theory Mardi Gra was as good as caught. On top of that, the Met had limited the amount of money the blackmailer would be able to draw at any one time. By drip-feeding it, they were forcing him to use the cashpoint more often and thus be guiding the undercover officers ever closer to him.

According to the police, it was five days from the start of the operation before Pearce finally came out. 'But when he did,' says Rees, 'our plan was activated and we had him in handcuffs within an hour.'

During those five days, the streets of west and south east London were flooded with surveillance teams watching hundreds of cash machines 24 hours a day.

'We were ready,' says Rees.

April 28, 6.14 p.m. The computer in New Scotland Yard sounded the alarm. A withdrawal had been made at the Midland bank in Ealing using the secret PIN. Mardi Gra had taken the bait. The surveillance teams in the Ealing area were alerted. But the machine Pearce had used wasn't one of those under surveillance. It was typical Mardi Gra luck.

Minutes ticked by. Back in the control room, Rees waited nervously to see if Mardi Gra would try again. A few more minutes elapsed. Then the computer's alarm went off again. Mardi Gra was just one mile from his first withdrawal.

'Suspect is on the Uxbridge Road in West Ealing! Does anyone have him?'

The control room was silent waiting for the reply.

'We have eyeball on suspects!'

Suspects? The National Crime Squad team on the ground confirmed. Suspects. There were two men. Two men dressed very strangely indeed. The description was read out. Now eyeball contact was made, Rees activated the second phase of the surveillance. The Mardi Gra men were to be followed.

'Got them!' Rees was jubilant, but knew the game was far from over. He wanted definitive proof that these men were the ones using Mardi Gra's cash cards. 'I was able to put a surveillance team around them and once I had that I was happy,' Rees reveals. The team had a far from easy job keeping their presence secret. 'The brothers were taking anti-surveillance measures. There were obvious attempts at disguise, which although looked bizarre, the measures they took were actually very effective because if we had have got them on camera, but not caught them, we would never have been able to recognise them from the pictures.'

The surveillance team watched the two men get into a

dark red Vauxhall Senator car and drive off. A mobile team moved in behind them. At a little before 6.40 p.m. the car pulled into Bridge Way just off Whitton High Street and parked up on a set of double yellow lines. Edgar and Ronald Pearce got out and made their way up the short distance to the High Street. Where Bridge Way joins the High Street is virtually opposite Keith Bray's electrical shop — the site of the fourteenth Mardi Gra attack. Edgar and Ronald began to walk down the High Street towards a Nationwide cash machine. The odd couple did indeed have bizarre disguises, disguises so strange in themselves, people turned to stare at them as they passed by. Both men wore identical fawn calf-length macs, identical beige trousers, gloves, wigs and dark glasses. Ronald had a checked hat pulled tightly down on his head; Edgar sported a white flat cap. Ronald had also dyed his trim beard black with mascara. Edgar was carrying a clipboard, on the back of which was fixed an A4 sized mirror, which he later said he used for 'counter surveillance' — he used it to look over his shoulder. The street was still busy with people, some of whom were heading for the fish and chip shop next to the cashpoint the brothers were making their way towards for a very different sort of takeaway.

Further down the street, a car containing more surveillance officers had parked up. One of the team inside began to record the scene with a video camera. That video was later to be leaked to the BBC's *Newsnight* programme, which broadcast the final dramatic minutes of the Mardi Gra campaign.

As the brothers reached the cash machine, Edgar placed the clipboard, mirror side down, onto the face of the cashpoint to block the camera he correctly suspected was hidden there. He began punching in numbers. As he was doing that, the pair's almost comical appearance continued to attract attention. One man performed two double takes as he strolled past them. Nearly two minutes passed, during which Edgar made two withdrawals of £250. All the time, the brothers were surrounded by undercover officers. 'It's the always the same story,' says Rees. 'These people — blackmailers — are exactly like bank robbers. They can spend months and months planning an operation, but when that money becomes available they become so focussed that's all they can see. Caution goes out the window. A surveillance officer can stand next to a bank robber during an operation and when that money is on the pavement they are totally focussed. Once they see the money, they get greedy and all caution goes.' While Edgar was withdrawing money, a man in a baseball cap came and stood right behind the brothers. Was he an undercover officer?

The cash machine coughed out its last payment and Edgar folded the cash tightly into the palm of his hand. Without speaking, the brothers turned from the machine. Edgar held the clipboard in front of his face as he walked away, occasionally staring out suspiciously from behind it. Ronald followed behind him, hands shoved deep into his pockets as the brothers made their way back towards the car. A little way up the street, Edgar lowered the clipboard and appeared to leaf through some papers clipped to it.

Back in the Operation Heath control room at New Scotland Yard, Rees was having the scene relayed to him by his officers. In front of him, the computers confirmed what Pearce had done at the machine and how much he had taken. Rees gave the order to move in.

On the ground, the undercover team decided to wait until Edgar and Ronald were back at their car. Mardi Gra had demonstrated his easy access to weapons and ammunition. The police didn't want to start a gun battle in the middle of a busy shopping street. The brothers reached the car and got in.

'Go! Go! Go!'

Undercover cars screeched into Bridge Way boxing in Edgar's Senator. Three officers ripped open the car's doors and hauled the stunned brothers out, splaying them face down onto the ground.

At 6.54 p.m., as Edgar lay pinned to the floor, he heard the words he had dreaded ever hearing. 'You are under arrest for demanding money with menaces and also firearms offences.' On the other side of the car, Ronald was receiving identical treatment. For the next half hour, the brothers and their car were meticulously searched. Their hats and wigs were pulled off, revealing the men beneath for the first time. Edgar was allowed to move to a sitting position, his hands on his head. Two officers moved in on either side of him and grabbed him under the armpits. 'Can I have your name sir,' said one.

'Pearce,' came the monosyllabic answer.

'Right Mr Pearce, I want you to stand up,' and without waiting for a reply, Pearce was hauled to his feet. As he did so, his glasses slipped so they were hanging half on, half off his face at a crazy angle. The officers made him stand with his arms spread out — he looked like he was being prepared for crucifixion. A white hooded evidence suit was produced and he was made to get into it. These suits ensure no forensic evidence such as fibres or traces of chemicals are lost and that the clothes are not contaminated by other sources. By 19.26, Pearce was stood on the pavement, suited up and looking for all the world like a giant white condom. A few yards away, other police officers were searching Ronald. One pulled at his hairpiece.

'Is that a wig you are wearing, Mr Pearce?'

'Yes.'

He looked crushed and humiliated. The officer half lifted the wig from Ronald's head for the benefit of a colleague filming the scene and then dropped it into a clear plastic evidence bag. Ronald looked like he just wanted the earth to open up beneath him and swallow him up. In the boot of the Senator, more disguises and makeup were found.

Rifling through Edgar's pockets, officers discovered notes detailing his reconnaissance intelligence. The notes included lists of cash machines which were not overlooked by security cameras and route plans detailing which roads had cameras on them and where. Inside Edgar's mac, there was a lead-lined wallet containing ten of the promotional Sainsbury's cards. Pearce was later to tell the police he put the lead in the wallet just in case the police had 'put something radioactive' in the cards. Inside the wallet there was also a scrap of paper with a number written on it. One of the officers got on the radio to Rees and read the number out to him. 'As soon as I got the message back that they were in possession of the cards and the PIN number, I knew we had them. I was the only one that knew the number. No other police officer knew that PIN number.'

That then is the official version of how the Mardi Gra bomber was finally caught. However, during the research for this book, a number of sources indicated this was not the entire story.

April 28 was a Tuesday, but sources close to the investigation have said during interviews for this book that Pearce was active the previous Friday, making his first withdrawal of £250 in £10 and £20 notes from a Barclays cashpoint in Ealing. Officers on the ground were unable to get to the machine before Pearce had left. He then struck again, still in Ealing.

Sources claim that by sheer co-incidence, an off-duty former Regional Crime Squad officer stopped off at the cashpoint while Pearce was making his withdrawal. Alerted by the same bizarre disguise that was to astonish the Operation Heath surveillance teams four days later, the officer decided to follow the oddly dressed man. The man drove straight back to Chiswick and Cambridge Road North.

An intense surveillance operation was mounted over that weekend with the house covered by mobile OPs and Pearce's car fitted with a hidden transmitter. Intelligence officers combed back through Pearce's life history, discovering only petty offences relating to being banned for drink driving and driving while disqualified. Two other occupants were also found to be living at the house. Were they connected to the Mardi Gra campaign?

Nothing happened over the weekend. Monday rolled on and still there was no significant activity. The house, under its invisible 24 hour guard, was quiet. By the time Tuesday came around, the Operation Heath team must have been coming to the conclusion that the officer's hunch had been wrong. The man seen at the cashpoint must have arrived just after the real Mardi Gra blackmailer had made a withdrawal. They would not be able to maintain the Cambridge Road North observation much longer as it was draining manpower from the wider pan-London operation. Then on the Tuesday evening, Pearce emerged. The OP teams alerted the control room.

'Suspect on the move.'

As Pearce drove away, the surveillance teams slipped in

behind him. Pearce drove first to collect his brother Ronald from his nearby flat in Chiswick High Road. The pair then drove off. They appeared to be scouting cashpoint locations. Machines in Southall and Hounslow were looked at, before the car made its way to Ealing.

If this version of events is accurate, it's ironic. The Met threw everything it had at the end stages of Operation Heath; more men than ever used in a single operation before; massive networks of remote surveillance cameras; cutting edge technology. All at a cost of millions of pounds. And yet it was the cheapest — and some say the best — investigative tool that may have finally ended Mardi Gra's campaign: good old-fashioned copper's instinct.

After the Pearce brothers had been hauled off to separate police stations for questioning, a team was dispatched to search Edgar's house. At just past 1 a.m., SO13 officers entered the building. The two sleeping male tenants on the first floor were quickly pulled from their beds and removed from the house. The explosives officers then began a cautious initial sweep of the flat. They found what they were looking for almost straight away. The officer leading the search made a hurried call back to New Scotland Yard, 'We've hit the jackpot, sir'.

It took four days to search 12, Cambridge Road North. Explosives officers worked their way painstakingly through the house. Everything found had to be checked to ensure that it was not in some way booby trapped. A forensic search like this starts logically at the front of the house and moves step by step inwards, room by room. Other officers do the same in the garden and in any other identified sites, such as Pearce's rented lock up garage a few streets away. What they discovered horrified them and the best way to appreciate that horror is to simply read the official Met inventory of what was discovered.

Items recovered from 12 Cambridge Road North
Two fully constructed and functional pipe bombs
Four partially constructed pipe bombs
One fully loaded functional shotgun device on a stand
Enough baseboard to construct fifteen more shotgun devices
272 twelve-gauge shotgun cartridges, plus modified and empty cut down cartridges
Two crossbows
Home-made bolts for the crossbows
A stun gun, disguised to look like a mobile phone
A loaded revolver with modified silencer and 10 modified cartridges to fit it
28 brass shell casings and 81 bullet tops awaiting assembly
50 rounds of .762 ammunition
Six butane gas cylinders with six gas igniters, one modified like the type used to activate the device planted on February 5, 1996
Various lengths of tubing
12 clockwork timers
39 video cassette boxes
25 spring-bolt mechanisms
Numerous 12 volt batteries
A huge selection of tools and other materials necessary to construct further devices

A team searching Ronald's flat recovered another stun gun.

It was only once the contents of Edgar Pearce's

residence were known that Rees began to appreciate just how dangerous Pearce had been. 'The real impact for me out of this was the threat the people of London were facing, albeit they didn't know it, from the devices that were in the home address. Take the stun gun for instance. These things are absolutely deadly. These things can kill. Pearce had disguised it to look like a mobile phone by sticking a calculator to its front and attaching an aerial to the top.'

The discoveries at Pearce's home added to what Sir Paul Condon would later call the Met's 'great sense of relief' that Mardi Gra 'had finally been taken off the streets. There was a real fear that sooner or later someone was going to be killed.' The contents of 12 Cambridge Road North reinforced just how close that prediction had come to becoming true.

Edgar Pearce was taken to a police station in Walworth for his interview, while Ronald was taken to Southwark. Their approach to their interviewers could not have been more different. While Edgar was 'very open and resigned', Ronald refused to talk to the police, maintaining a 'no comment' stance throughout.

Edgar was more than just 'open'. There is a slang expression which perfectly described what he did over the next three days of interviews — he spilled his guts. It were as though he was glad it was all over and at last he could get it all off his chest; his motives, the planning, the execution, the cash cards. The police couldn't shut him up.

His manner of speaking and explanation were disjointed and awkward. He spoke as he thought, sentences spilling out one on top of another following his stream of consciousness. Take this example from the first interview, where he describes the first attacks.

'I chose the original six branches due to the access

being possible without video surveillance. Those sent through the post were just picked out of the phone book. I don't recall those details except west London. I don't know why except that I had a Yellow Pages. I got the idea for the devices from another TV programme. This involved spring loaded cartridges. If you look at the original ones, they were a slight extension of that idea.

'I have handled guns but I was able to work out the construction for myself. It was very simplistic . . . I knew this would end up like a firework and not much force would result. I didn't have any intention to injure anyone.

'I tested the devices at home. No damage was caused. I primed the cartridge to test the alignment. I didn't detonate a live cartridge. Regarding people opening the mail which I sent, I suppose I wanted the damage to be as minimal as possible. Six branches received devices with a demand letter. I didn't think the response was valid. It was an extortion attempt. I didn't pursue it then because they invited me to meet up and collect a bag of money. I didn't want to do this as I had already suggested a credit card plan which has never changed. Ten cards required International access. I originally asked for it to go in a video magazine. I was looking for a low circulation so that the inserts could be put in.'

These statements from the beginning of his confession are also interesting because they show up a feature that was to crop up time and again during the interviews. As we saw in the previous chapter, despite being almost overly frank in his revelations, when Pearce got to an area where the subject turns round to the harm caused or the potential threat posed by his devices, he is always defensive, quick to mitigate for himself. 'I suppose I wanted the damage to be as minimal as possible'. 'I didn't have any intention to injure anyone.'

Throughout, he refuses to accept that he intended to

hurt people; he also refuses to accept that if anyone was hurt, it was his fault. He tries to brush any suggestion away by blaming anything other than himself — it was an old man's fault for disturbing him at Forest Hill; it was the fault of Sainsbury's guards for not 'being on their toes' and finding his devices before they exploded; it was the shoppers' fault for 'stealing' his shopping bag bombs before the security guards could find them; it was the device's fault for not exploding the way they did during his testing.

The only thing Edgar Pearce would not talk about was his brother's involvement. Asked what his brother was doing there, he simply says, 'My brother was with me because it took three to four years for me to get to this position and I was elated. I wanted to show him some real magic.' So why was Ronald in disguise too?

Wasn't he suspicious about what Pearce was up to? Wasn't he worried? Much to the police's frustration, Pearce would say nothing further on Ronald's involvement.

To this day neither Edgar nor Ronald have ever spoken about what Ronald was doing there on April the 28th in a wig, his beard coloured with mascara, wearing that ludicrous disguise clothing.

Ronald has, however, tried to sell his version of events to newspapers and to this author. After almost two months of trying to contact Ronald, he called one Saturday morning to reveal that no-one from the Pearce family — Maureen, Nicola, himself or his girlfriend Sonia Bickham — would talk unless they were paid. He said he wanted 'something of value' in return for 'the lurid details.' 'That is the bottom line,' he said. The family was 'looking to cover our costs and debts and get something for the future.'

He was also aware that as a convicted criminal and a blood relative of Edgar the law would not allow him to profit directly from the crime. But he had a solution to that. 'We will take the money in a Swiss bank account or even in Thai Bhat,' he said. 'Then we can talk turkey. Everyone in the scenario will tell all. The real story makes the Brinks Mat robbery look like small beer. It involved £9.7 million per year anywhere in the world — people thought he had brought plastic money to its knees.'

All he would say about his involvement was, 'I got stuck with one of Edgar's rotten stun guns that he left in the house. The police always knew I was innocent. I was a sword of Damocles held over Edgar's head to get a guilty plea.'

Not surprisingly, the police have a different view of Ronald's 'no comment' interviews and of Edgar's stubborn silence over this matter. 'It was all part of this bargaining process,' says Rees. 'It was obvious to us, that he wanted to make sure that Ronald would walk free.'

The brothers had been under arrest for only a day when the story leaked out to the media. 12, Cambridge Road North was soon besieged by reporters, photographers and television camera crews. With Jeff Rees fully occupied with the brothers' questioning, Deputy Assistant Commissioner John Grieve, head of SO13, was nominated to make a public statement. The statement was brief, confirming the brother's names and ages and giving precious few details of the operation that had led to the arrest. The next day, the arrest of the Pearce brothers became public knowledge and that evening, the brothers were charged with conspiracy to blackmail Barclays Bank, conspiracy to blackmail Sainsbury's and conspiracy to possess firearms with intent to endanger life.

At 10 a.m. on Friday April 30, they appeared at Horseferry Road Magistrates' court in central London.

During the 30-minute hearing, Ronald appeared nervous, twitching whenever he was referred to. Edgar, dressed in an unflattering red and grey tracksuit, maintained what was to become a familiar expressionless façade. Watching from the public gallery were Edgar's estranged wife, Maureen, and their daughter Nicola. It was to be the first and last time they appeared at court to witness the fate of Edgar. Sonia Bickham had fled her flat when the news of the arrests first came out and was never to come to court.

Nicola's Pearce's shock at her father's arrest was absolute. She could not comprehend that Edgar Pearce could be Mardi Gra. Her father? A blackmailer? A bomber? Who could believe that about their father?

'I found out about he had been arrested just before the news broke in a phone call from my family,' she said. 'I can't believe that my father had anything to do with these bombings. He's a gentle man. He wouldn't do anything like this. He's not screwed up in the head at all.

'Dad was always a bit of a recluse, but he was more just quiet than anything. He never had any guns or anything like that and he's never been in trouble with the law. He's just a normal 60- year-old man. I keep thinking somebody is going to tell me that it is a case of mistaken identity.'

At the end of the hearing, Ronald was remanded in custody for seven days; Edgar was to be taken back to Walworth police station for another 48 hours of questioning. A day later, he appeared before a special Saturday sitting at Bow Street magistrates' court and he too was remanded in custody. Neither men wasted their time applying for bail.

For nearly twelve months, the men were held on remand as Category A prisoners — the category used for the country's most dangerous criminals such as IRA terrorists, murderers, armed robbers and serial rapists. Rodney was sent to HMP High Down in Surrey, where, he says he 'spent seven months incommunicado from Edgar.' He describes his prison experience as 'a real eye opener. I'd never been banged up before.' In High Down he was kept in virtual isolation as there were only two other Cat A prisoners locked up there. Edgar was sent to HMP Belmarsh, one of the toughest prisons in the country. Around 70 per cent of its inmates are Cat A. They include the notorious gangland bosses, the Adams Family.

Over the next year, the brothers were to make numerous court appearances as the case against them was prepared. A total of twenty charges relating to the campaign were listed. Matters were complicated by Edgar, who proceeded to hire and fire a succession of solicitors as the case moved closer to trial. After seven months in High Down, Rodney was moved to Belmarsh so he was close to London for the start of the trial. He was held in Houseblock 4 and was shocked by the regime at the prison, describing it as 'dismal and oppressive'.

Finally, a court date was listed. The brothers were committed to stand trial at the Central Criminal Court on February 5, 1999.

Careless Whispers

Welcome to the Mardi Gra Experience

The rumours began circulating early in the week. They came from inside New Scotland Yard and they came from high up.

The bombers were going to plead guilty on Friday.

Crime reporters from most national newspapers and the major television channels were given the nod by the Met's press office. Others were tipped off by those working close to the case who had been leaking information to favoured journalists. Editors began forward planning. By Thursday, most had their backgrounders planned and their reporters prepped. The rumours were also fizzing through police circles; 'the word' was popping out all over the place.

A senior source from the Flying Squad confirmed more

details. Yes, there were going to be guilty pleas. Edgar Pearce was going to put forward a mitigation of diminished responsibility. 'He was run over in 1994,' confided the source. 'His defence are going to say he's not been right in the head ever since.'

The Met was swinging into action, making preparations for the big day. A triumphal press conference was planned for the Friday afternoon, to follow the morning's hearing. The Commissioner, Sir Paul Condon, was to take the conference himself along with chief investigating officer Jeff Rees. After the humiliations heaped on the Met by the disastrous enquiry into the murder of black teenager Stephen Lawrence and the corruption scandals plaguing the Flying Squad, this was a public relations exercise that couldn't be missed. More than that, it had to be a high-profile example of a successful investigation into a major, complex series of crimes.

A comprehensive briefing of Operation Heath was written and prepared for journalists. There was to be a table of exhibits and a question and answer session in the Met's conference room. 'You don't want to miss this,' assured one press officer.

Friday morning rolled around. It was a cold, miserable day. Rogue drops of rain spattered down here and there, threatening to turn themselves into a proper downpour. An icy wind gusted down the Old Bailey, the street which has given the Central Criminal Court its more familiar name.

The Old Bailey has been the venue for some of the most celebrated trials in English legal history. Oscar Wilde was tried there, Dr Crippen was sentenced to death there and the Yorkshire Ripper's murderous reign was finally ended there. It is also the venue for all major terrorist trials held on the UK mainland. Today around 1,500 cases a year are heard. And it is to this place Edgar and Ronald Pearce were to be brought to face their accusers.

By 9.15 a.m. the first camera crews and photographers were already in place. They all wanted to get shots of the prison van coming in and to bag a prime place to catch the lawyers, police and members of the Pearce family (if they turned up) coming out of court after the hearing was over.

An hour or so later, it was beginning to get crowded inside the Old Bailey. Outside Court Eight, three distinct cliques developed — the police, newspaper reporters and television journalists all huddled in their separate groups. Gossip was exchanged, cigarettes smoked, endless calls made on mobile phones.

At 11 a.m. the pack filed into court, the journalists settling into the press benches on the far side of the room, the police in two rows of chairs set exactly opposite the press benches on the other side of the court.

The crime reporters chatted amongst themselves, swapping tit bits of information.

There is a competitive edge to this kind of banter. You want everyone to know you have that extra-special something, the something that will make your story so much better than all the rest, but you don't want to let on what (if, in reality, anything) that extra-special something is. It makes for cryptic, amusing conversation. A lot of the talk was about how unlikely a pair of bombers the Pearce brothers were. It was nearly a year since their arrest and yet there was still a sense of incredulity that the story that had kept the nation fascinated for nearly four years had its genesis with two elderly men from Chiswick. 'At the end of the day,' one old hand remarked, 'a pair of pensioners weren't exactly high on the police's list of suspects.'

What was generally agreed, however, was that, barring

the death of King Hussein of Jordan who was reported to be on a life-support machine after a failed bone marrow transplant, this story would be the front page lead for most papers the next day and the lead story on all the evening news bulletins.

The Pearce brothers were that morning facing a total of twenty charges. On his own, Edgar faced all twenty — nine of blackmail against Barclays and Sainsbury's, three of causing actual bodily harm (ABH), one of wounding with intent, one of causing an explosion, one of intending to cause an explosion, one charge of illegally possessing an 'improvised shotgun device' with intent to commit blackmail, another charge of illegally possessing an 'improvised shotgun device', this time with intent to endanger life, one charge of possessing explosives and two charges of illegally possessing prohibited weapons.

Ronald was jointly charged with nine of those offences — four counts of blackmailing Sainsbury's, one offence of ABH, one charge of wounding with intent, one count of possessing the 'improvised shotgun device' with intent to endanger life, one count of possessing explosives and one charge of possessing a prohibited weapon.

Edgar came into the dock first, followed a little way behind by Ronald. Edgar had sprouted an untidy growth of grey beard since his last appearance. As usual, he looked the more pensive of the two, his arms held stiffly at his side.

'All stand.'

Judge Neil Denison, who as The Common Serjeant of London is the city's second most senior judge, entered. The court settled and waited with anticipation.

The clerk addressed the defendants.

'Are you Edgar Eugene Pearce?'

'Yes.'

'Are you Ronald Russell Pearce?'

'Yes.'

Both men spoke up in firm voices. The clerk began to outline the number of charges they faced.

She read the first charge — that sometime between the first and the ninth of December, Edgar Eugene Pearce had blackmailed Barclays Bank.

'How do you plead?' she asked.

This was it. The beginning of the end.

'Not guilty.'

There was an audible groan from the press benches. Earlier, a few reporters had been discussing the worst possible outcome, that one brother was going to plead guilty and the other not guilty, leaving the case in limbo while one was tried for crimes (or some crimes) for which the other had already admitted. It looked like the worst case scenario was about to fulfilled.

The clerk began rattling through the indictments. Edgar pleaded not guilty to nine charges before the clerk reached the first joint charge, that of blackmailing Sainsbury's.

Edgar, true to form, entered a not guilty plea.

'Ronald Russell Pearce, how do you plead?'

'Not guilty.'

And there it was. It was going to be a full Old Bailey trial.

It took the clerk ten minutes to read out all the charges. When she finished, the judge was informed the parties had discussed and agreed on April 7 as a day when they could start the trial.

The judge agreed. April 7 it was to be.

The news schedules were rearranged, the backgrounders filed away for a later date. Instead of making a front page, the story was relegated to the inside of the paper, a few paragraphs languishing at the bottom of the news pages.

King Hussein of Jordan died 48 hours later.

April 7, 1999.

Edgar and Ronald Pearce finally entered the dock at noon after a morning of delays and behind-the-scenes legal arguments. Just days before the hearing, Edgar had yet again sacked his solicitor and leading counsel, leaving only a junior barrister to face the city's most senior judge, The Recorder of London, Judge Michael Hyam. A new solicitor had been appointed, but without leading counsel it would be impossible to progress the trial beyond the pleas. Nevertheless, the trial started and the brothers stood to answer the charges against them.

The first charge against Edgar was read out. He replied without hesitation.

'Guilty'.

Mardi Gra had finally admitted defeat. Soon, another nineteen guilty pleas stood alongside his first.

Next to him, Ronald waited his turn. To the first charge, possession of the stun gun found in a cupboard in his flat, he pled guilty. But he would go no further and entered not guilty pleas to the remaining charges. The prosecuting barrister, Nigel Sweeney QC, stood to address the judge. Ronald's pleas presented the Crown with a difficult dilemma, he said. Ronald Pearce had been observed and filmed accompanying Edgar as he collected blackmail money deposited by Sainsbury's. There was no doubt he had been there in Whitton with his brother on that day. But going beyond that, to prove he had been a part of the blackmail plan itself would require a full trial. And with Edgar refusing to talk about his brother, and Ronald refusing to comment at all, the Crown had to weigh up whether it was in the public interest to pursue an long and expensive trial, particularly given Edgar's guilty pleas to all charges. After long consideration, he said, the Crown had decided to offer no evidence on the remaining charges against Ronald, although a charge of conspiracy to blackmail Sainsbury's would lie on file.

For possession of the stun gun, Judge Hyam sentenced Ronald to twelve months in jail. But as he had spent that long in prison on remand, this meant Ronald was from that moment a free man. He was led from the dock by a prison officer, leaving Edgar alone. As he walked away, Ronald neither looked at, nor spoke to, his brother.

In the normal course of events, the trial should have moved to mitigation and sentencing. Mitigation is when defence counsel attempts to explain any extraordinary circumstances that might have led a defendant to commit their crimes and offer any help or assistance they had given to the police as a reason for a reduced sentence. But, as with the last five years of Edgar Pearce's life, things were not normal. With no QC to lead his case, the case could not proceed. A QC Pearce approved of had been found, the court was told, but would not be available until Monday the 12th. Judge Hyam adjourned the case until then.

Ronald emerged from the Old Bailey a short time later to run the gauntlet of reporters, photographers and camera crews. Flanked by his legal team he tried to scurry away from the descending mob.

'Are you happy to be out?' a reporter shouted to him.

'I am indeed yes. But no further comment.'

'What's your brother's state of mind today?'

'He's very sad.'

With that, Ronald was whisked away. Later that day he was reunited with Sonia. That night, they walked to a restaurant near their flat and shared their first meal for a year. Still pursued by journalists, Ronald maintained an embarrassed silence, covering his face. As she hurried along beside him, Sonia would only say that Ronald felt 'tremendous' to be free again and added, 'We're going home, we're going to have a meal, champagne and then sex.'

While his brother was enjoying his freedom, Edgar was taken back to Belmarsh. It's extremely doubtful if his evening was quite as enjoyable.

Mad or Bad?

Welcome to the Mardi Gra Experience

April 12.

The court sat once more before Judge Michael Hyam, this time to decide Edgar Pearce's fate. In the five intervening days between this hearing and Pearce's earlier guilty plea, his choice of leading counsel, Nadine Radford QC, had undergone a crash course in the Mardi Gra Experience. She had had to absorb a ludicrous amount of information, contained in dozens of files, in far too short a time period. However, the court was not going to tolerate any further delays — not even to allow respected QCs to do their homework. There was, however, one insurmountable problem. The one witness Mrs Radford wanted to call was in Japan.

Nevertheless, Mrs Radford rose and outlined her application to the judge — for a section 38 order to made under the 1983 Mental Health Act with a view to eventually making a section 37 order. Pearce's opening move was made, indicating his intentions and confirming the rumours which had been circulating for days. He was going to try and argue that he had committed his crimes because he was suffering from some sort of mental disorder and not because he was simply a greedy, malicious criminal.

In other words, he was mad, not bad.

Courts have various powers to sentence anyone with a mental disorder to a hospital sentence in a psychiatric unit rather than a jail sentence. The problem is that it's open to abuse. Someone may be able to buck the system and by faking symptoms end up in hospital rather than jail. With the detention of those sentenced to hospital terms reviewed every six months with a view to releasing those who genuinely no longer present a danger to the public, a convincing faker — or indeed someone in whom a genuine diagnostic error has been made — could end up escaping a lengthy jail sentence and serving only a minimal term in the less harsh environment of a hospital, albeit a secure one.

In order to allow the maximum certainty to be attached to a diagnosis before sentence, the 1983 Mental Health Act makes provision for an interim order to be made before sentence. This is made under section 38 of the Act and allows a defendant to be assessed by the hospital he will eventually end up in if a mental disorder is confirmed.

In effect, it gives the court a second chance if a mistake has been made. For the judge to make an order under this section, the defendant must have already been convicted of an offence for which the option of a full hospital order would be available. Pearce had admitted his guilt in several offences which would, if a mental disorder could be proved during the twelve weeks allowed by the interim section 38 order, qualify for a full order to be made under section 37 of the Act.

The other requirement for a section 38 order is that two doctors — one of whom must be from the intended hospital of referral — have to give evidence that the defendant is suffering from one of four conditions; a mental illness, a psychopathic disorder, mental impairment or severe mental impairment. It was to be argued that Pearce was suffering from a mental illness. Doubtless Pearce's lawyers would have warned him of how difficult a path this was to pursue. The judge was bound to be highly resistant to such an application because of the further delays it would build into the case. But the stakes were high — success meant incarceration in a hospital; failure meant looking forward to life in a maximum security jail. The problem in this case was to be getting the doctors physically into court.

Two psychiatric reports had been prepared prior to Pearce's guilty plea. The most important was by Dr Peter Fenwick, a neuro-psychiatrist. The doctor had been given access to Pearce's GP notes, hospital records and CT scans relating to the 1992 incident which left Pearce hospitalised after a suspected stroke. In preparation for this case, further detailed scans of Pearce's brain had been carried out in January 1999 using Magnetic Resonance Imaging (MRI).

Mrs Radford prepared to outline her case, but first had to explain to the judge that in order to make her case, she needed the direct testimony of Dr Fenwick. Unfortunately, Dr Fenwick was attending a conference in Japan and would not be back in the country for another two days. However, Mrs Radford had spent the weekend on the phone to Dr Fenwick in Japan and had received a crash course in neuro-psychiatry. With the court's permission, she intended to take the case as far as she could and then ask for a two-day adjournment to allow Dr Fenwick to give his evidence in person. Judge Hyam was obviously rankled by this. The court had sat that day expecting to be able to proceed with sentencing. This was yet another delay. It was for Mrs Radford to try and convince him that he actually needed to hear Dr Fenwick's evidence.

Essentially the defence case was this; that Pearce, following a fall in 1992 which was probably caused by a stroke, had developed a mental illness which had led him to become the Mardi Gra bomber. Mrs Radford continued by saying that Sonia Bickham, Ronald's girlfriend, had made a statement saying she had witnessed a 'great personality change' after the fall.

The fall in 1992 had been a serious one. Mrs Radford told the court that Pearce believed the fall occurred after he was hit by a bike. Other witnesses had said he simply collapsed in the street. Whatever the cause, as Pearce was being taken to hospital, he suffered a Grand Mal epileptic seizure in the ambulance and in the days following his admission had continued to fit. As a result of the fall, he had also severely fractured his shoulder, an injury which needed surgery and left him in 'considerable pain' requiring strong painkilling medication in the weeks following the injury. It was not clear at this stage, added Mrs Radford, if Pearce had suffered a stroke as a result of the fit, or had suffered a fit first which caused a stroke and led to more fitting caused by an internal bleed into the brain.

Mrs Radford said the medical evidence showed that as a consequence of this incident, Pearce had suffered a severe bleed into the left frontal lobe of his brain. In addition, Pearce was suffering from hypertension (high blood pressure), which had led to further degradation of the frontal lobe. As a result, she said, Pearce was now thought to be suffering from a rare condition called Binswanger's disease.

This was the moment the prosecution had probably been waiting for with some apprehension. The day before, the *Observer* newspaper had run an article under the headline 'Mardi Gra bomber "suffering from rare brain disease" ', which appeared to be based on a leak from a member of Pearce's defence team or family. The article stated the defence would be arguing that Pearce carried out his campaign while suffering from Binswanger's, which the *Observer* defined as 'a progressive deterioration of the brain for which there is no known cure.' It also quoted 'a medical source close to Pearce's legal team' as saying, 'he's not insane, because intellectually he knows the difference between right and wrong. But the part of his brain that can relate to the emotions of others has been wiped out, so he has no moral sense.'

And in court number seven, Mrs Radford appeared to be following the line that Pearce had suffered brain damage which had led to mental illness. Neuro psychometric testing had, she said, proved the damage.

So that was the history. But how did that affect Pearce now and why should his medical condition enable him to avoid a prison sentence? And what exactly was Binswanger's disease? Glancing occasionally at the file before her, Mrs Radford waded deeper into the medical evidence.

Pearce's problem at the moment was that he was still suffering from hypertension. This was causing rapid acceleration of the destruction of his brain and it was this which constituted the Binswanger's disease. While medication to control the hypertension was being given in prison, the treatment was not adequate to control his deterioration. 'If he remains within the prison confines, because of his medical condition, it will cause a progression of his psychiatric problems leading to dementia.' The progressive dementia would cause Pearce to behave 'inappropriately'. This in turn might lead him into conflict with other prisoners. If he were assaulted as a result, there was a risk of a further stroke or even death.

Judge Hyam was clearly having a difficult time swallowing this. What, he wanted to know, made Pearce so different from other prisoners who have high blood pressure? After all, they didn't all need to go to Broadmoor and if at a later stage they did need hospital treatment, the Home Secretary had the power to authorise a transfer.

Mrs Radford was clearly frustrated by the lack of her expert witness. It was not her job to try and present complex medical evidence or to offer explanations about expert findings. Yet, as she found herself landed with the job by default, she tried again.

'It's not a question of him suffering from something like HIV or a heart condition. It goes beyond the physical dimension and into the mental condition and the difficulty of dealing with the mental condition in a prison environment. He is prone to be demented. While in Broadmoor, they would be able to treat the physical symptoms of his condition and work with Mr Pearce to address his thinking processes in order to train him to deal with situations more effectively so as to lessen the risk of further stroke.'

There was no question of Pearce faking the illness, she argued. The symptoms were completely in line with the damage that had been shown. She added that Pearce was also 'beginning to get an idea of how he got himself into this predicament.'

She had taken her argument as far as she could.

Judge Hyam took a moment to contemplate what he

had heard. He looked first at Pearce, who sat implacably between two bored-looking prison officers and then down at the pages of notes he had taken during Mrs Radford's presentation to the court.

'There are,' he said eventually, 'scanty grounds for thinking that a section 38 and ultimately a section 37 order would be appropriate in this case, but it is difficult for me, though unwilling, to resist the force of the application. The defendant should feel that everything is being done and has been done that preserve his rights to a fair hearing and on that ground alone — without I hope giving any cause for hope to the defendant that a hospital order will be the outcome — I am prepared to grant an adjournment until Wednesday so I can hear Dr Fenwick.'

Wednesday April 14, 1999

Dr Peter Fenwick is one of Britain's leading psychiatrists. A consultant neuro-psychiatrist, he specialises in psychiatric conditions which are the consequence of neurological diseases or damage. During 40-odd years of practice, he has run an epilepsy clinic at the country's top psychiatric hospital, the Maudsley Hospital in south London and currently runs a research unit at Broadmoor, a neuro-psychiatric clinic at the Radcliffe Hospital in Oxford and is also a senior lecturer at the Institute of Psychiatry. He has been an expert witness in a number of leading cases which hinged on the defendant's mental condition at the time of a criminal act and is also as an authority on sleep disorders.

He had been commissioned by Pearce's defence team to try and find a reason why Pearce had done what he had done. Was Pearce mad or bad? And given Dr Fenwick's expertise in epilepsy, the defence also wanted to explore the possibility of an epileptic cause. What follows here is based on the evidence Dr Fenwick gave at court and a subsequent interview with him.

From the outset, Dr Fenwick was convinced it was something other than pure criminality which had led Pearce to become the Mardi Gra Bomber. 'If you have someone who has been normal and then goes on a bombing rampage at the age of 60 then clearly there's something wrong.'

The first job was to examine Pearce's medical history, in particular his collapse and subsequent hospitalisation in 1992. All his criminal actions appeared to stem from this moment in time, so a thorough investigation needed to be mounted to establish exactly what had happened and what the consequences of that episode could have been for Pearce's mental health.

Certainly in the ten years preceding 1992, Pearce had been a heavy drinker. His drinking had been gradually increasing over the years, going from one bottle of wine a day to two bottles. Sometimes, Pearce managed to consume a staggering six bottles of wine a day — this is the equivalent of him drinking around one and-a-half times the recommended weekly intake for a man in just one day. And he didn't just confine his drinking to wine, but also consumed strong lager and spirits, particularly gin, and often all in the same session. When his liver was tested following his arrest it showed clearly abnormal function, a sign it was dying from the abuse it had been subjected to over the years.

But Pearce had an equally serious and equally hidden medical problem — hypertension. Whether this was caused by his drinking or due to other factors was something the judge took particular interest in. In Dr Fenwick's opinion, 'The judge was very much for the drinking being the cause, because what he wanted to do was see this as an imposed illness due to alcohol. In law, alcohol is recklessness and therefore any of the effects of alcohol a person has brought on themselves and so the judge could send Pearce to prison and not to hospital because Pearce himself had caused his illness.' Fenwick argued strongly against this, pointing out that there were many other possible factors, including well-documented genetic tendencies in this area.

However, even if the causes of Pearce's hypertension were not clear, the effects of the illness were. The hypertension was damaging the tiny blood vessels in Pearce's brain. This, in Dr Fenwick's opinion, caused a stroke which was behind the 1992 fall. The suspicion that Pearce had epilepsy which in turn led to the stroke was unfounded, he said. 'Pearce had a fit at the time when he fell to the ground with the stroke, then he had a fit in the ambulance and then he had some fits in the hospital. These can be explained by the stroke — he's bleeding into the brain. He had seizures from a precipitating cause. He didn't have spontaneous seizures — they were related directly to the bleed. He didn't have epilepsy.'

The stroke caused a large bleed into the left frontal lobe of Pearce's brain. The significance of the location of the bleed was a crucial factor in Pearce's case. Tests carried out in Charing Cross Hospital, where Pearce was taken after the stroke, showed the extent of the damage caused by the bleed as did subsequent tests carried out in preparation of his defence. The latter MRI scans also showed small white patches throughout Pearce's brain — indicative of small vessel disease. 'What this means,' says Dr Fenwick, 'is that all the small blood vessels in his brain are seizing up and when they seize up you get an area of the brain beyond them that dies. The brain becomes full of little holes and you can pick this up on the scan. This is what happened to Pearce. As a result all functions of mind began to deteriorate.

'So that's the 1992 injury. But to get to that point he

must have had the beginnings of hypertensive vascular disease of the brain otherwise he wouldn't have had his stroke. The hypertensive disease is causing damage, the stroke causes more damage — so he's doubly damaged.'

However in 1992, Pearce's doctors had presumed he was suffering from epilepsy and that the stroke had been a consequence of that. Pearce was discharged from hospital and sent home with medication for epilepsy and strong painkillers for the shoulder injury. The progressing vascular disease and the damage it was causing was left unchecked.

Once back at Cambridge Road North, the medical evidence showed Pearce sank into depression and became reclusive. The depression stemmed from two factors. Firstly, the damage to his left frontal lobe. Research has shown that damage to this area of the brain can be a primary factor in the causes of depression. Indeed, depression among brain-injured patients is a well-documented phenomenon and lesions in the frontal lobe correlate very highly with episodes of depression. Secondly, following his return home, Pearce found himself totally isolated. Unable to work because of his injuries, in constant pain from his broken shoulder and lonely following the spilt from his wife, Pearce essentially vegetated. He was also told by his doctors that he only had two years to live. This of course could have been couched in the term 'if you keep on drinking this amount you are going to die.' However, in his current state, Pearce managed to convince himself that he was terminally ill. There was no medical follow-up of any sort except by a neurologist specialising in epilepsy. As Pearce did not have epilepsy, and the specialist would not have had the appropriate psychiatric training to identify Pearce's real problem, Pearce was left to drift off on his own.

'In a sense,' explained Dr Fenwick, 'he felt he was just

hanging about waiting to die. So he became very despondent and watched a lot of television and did nothing very much. And it was in that context that he entered into a bizarre fantasy world.'

The causative factors behind the evolution of Pearce's 'fantasy world' were to be revealed by an extensive series of tests carried out by Dr Fenwick while Pearce was on remand at HMP Belmarsh.

Three types of test were performed: MRI scans, which reveal brain structure, an electroencephalograph (EEG), which reveals the electrical function of the brain and a series of neuro-psychometric tests, which reveal the cognitive function of the brain. The MRI scan showed the physical damage to Pearce's brain. The EEG showed results which Dr Fenwick describes as being 'very abnormal'. Then came the neuro-psychometric testing.

A total of eleven tests were carried out to assess Pearce's cognitive functioning looking at areas including vocabulary, arithmetic and comprehension. Other tests in the series were designed to assess how the damage to Pearce's frontal lobe had affected him. Frontal lobe tests show whether a person is able to make executive decisions, the ability to change a decision or way of behaving based on the information the brain is receiving. One of these tests was a card test where the subject is required to sort cards according to their shape, colour or by a number printed on each card.

When the test starts the subject is given a specific task — say, to sort the cards into different piles according to their shape. Each time this is done correctly the tester says 'right'. As the test progresses, the tester will suddenly change the rules and tell the subject to now sort by colour. Each time this is done correctly, the tester says 'right'. If a mistake is made, the tester says 'wrong'. Pearce failed this test miserably.

Dr Fenwick explained, 'The patient is sorting by shape and you then tell him to sort by colour. When he puts the next card down in the shape pile you say 'wrong'. Now the patient knows he is wrong, but people with frontal lobe damage can't change their thinking, so they go on making mistakes even though they've been told it's wrong. They will keep putting cards in the colour pile when they clearly should be trying the other piles.'

From these tests, Dr Fenwick was able to establish that the damage to Pearce's frontal lobes had affected his ability to relate to 'the outside world'. On top of that, Pearce was suffering a progressive dementia, which further inhibited his ability to cope with normal social situations.

And there was one more give-away clue which Dr Fenwick discovered during the testing process. 'Pearce was unable to understand what the effect of what he was saying and doing had on other people. You could see this from the way that when he was questioned by the police, he had just no idea of how he was incriminating himself with everything that he said.

'For example, he would correct the police officers on the way he had made the devices. They would say "What, like this?" and he would say "No, no, no, I did it like this." He just kept incriminating himself.'

So, the argument went, after the 1992 stroke, Pearce was brain damaged. This caused depression and also inhibited his ability to judge the effect of his words and deeds on others. He was also entering the first phase of dementia and continued to drink heavily, thereby accelerating the damage to his brain.

But what about the mysterious Binswanger's disease which had caught everyone's attention in court? Dr Fenwick gave a surprising answer. 'I don't know where that came from,' he said and then quickly added, 'well, I do know. It was something he [Pearce] came up with and handed to his defence.' This was an interesting revelation, because a month before the trail, Pearce's wife Maureen had faxed a rambling letter to the *Observer* on Pearce's behalf. In the letter, she (and Pearce) appeared to blame Dr Fenwick for the diagnosis. The letter read, 'Edgar Pearce — the alleged Mardi-Gras [sic] man is allegedly full of galloping Binswanger's disease and Asperger's syndrome too. These types of dementia-related, amnesiac conditions and behaviour are due to a stroke in 1992. A top international neuro-psychiatrist's prognosis is an insidious, non-too-distant personality crash [sic].'

Did this mean that Pearce didn't have Binswanger's disease and had been cynically trying to come up with some exotic sounding condition in a last desperate attempt to get himself off the hook, only to change his mind at the last minute? It wasn't quite as simple as that. Binswanger's disease is a recognised condition, but many doctors believe there is little or no difference between it and other forms of multi-infarct dementia. An infarct is a piece of tissue destroyed by the deprivation of blood. Pearce did have multi-infarct dementia, said Dr Fenwick, but to definitely say it was of a type which could be distinctly classified as Binswanger's was difficult. With Binswanger's disease, there is an association with very high blood pressure, which Pearce had. Also, the evidence of the strokes is said to be more obvious and the decline of the patient's mental state more rapid than some other multi-infarct dementias. In Dr Fenwick's opinion, all that could definitely be said was that Pearce was suffering from multi-infarct dementia, a condition which accounts for around fifteen per cent of all dementias.

Which left one question begging. There are many

people who have strokes, many people who have brain damage and many people who suffer from multi-infarct dementias. Yet they don't suddenly turn into bombers or criminals. What was so special about Pearce's case?

Sitting in his darkened front room, depressed, isolated and in pain, Pearce spent his days watching endless television. Weeks, months rolled by, during which his mental state deteriorated. The television became virtually his only source of contact with the outside world. It also smoothed away the dull hours of each day and distracted him from the pain and discomfort he found himself enduring. As we now know, it was during this time that he watched a documentary about the life and crimes of Rodney Whitchelo, the Heinz baby food blackmailer. Pearce admits the programme fascinated him and he begin to try and work out why and where Whitchelo had gone wrong. At some point during this process, fascination became fantasy.

He could do better than Whitchelo. It would be easy. But because of the damage to his frontal lobe, what was missing was the 'safety mechanism' which most people possess that applies the brakes before fantasies get out of control.

'So if he gets an excellent idea, then there's no reason why he shouldn't go ahead with it because he's unable to think in what way it would be viewed by society as a whole. He isn't relating to people with minds like that,' says Dr Fenwick. 'He couldn't understand what other people would think of him. He constructs a situation without getting the feedback from other people of how he's behaving.'

But, there was a problem with this theory, a problem which Judge Hyam clearly identified. Dr Fenwick admitted and Pearce accepted that although he might not have been able to perceive society's objection to his actions, he knew that what he was doing was wrong. And inevitably this fact scuppered any chance Pearce had of being recognised as mentally ill by the court. In law, the test to decide if a defendant is mad or bad was established in the case of M'Naghten. The rule is that a person is deemed 'mad' if they did not know what they were doing or, if they did, they didn't realise it was wrong.

Dr Fenwick says, 'Pearce was clearly not M'Naghten mad. But he is mad in the sense that he did not know what other people were thinking. He's certainly not bad because for 60-odd years he didn't do anything like this at all. So something happened after the stroke. He cannot think. He's brain damaged and mad.'

After Fenwick gave evidence, Judge Hyam made an immediate ruling and began by accepting the substantial evidence of Pearce's brain damage. 'The defendant is evidently brain damaged. It's also fair to say that he is in the early stages of dementia,' he started.

But that was as good as it was going to get. Judge Hyam continued, 'His blood pressure can quite clearly be treated in prison, the epilepsy [which Pearce didn't have] can quite clearly be treated in prison as can his physical needs from a medical point of view. If his medical situation deteriorates while in prison, there is provision for the Secretary of State to order hospital treatment.

'I have considered this very carefully — there is in fact no need for further assessment. Under the circumstances the application for an assessment under section 38 is refused.'

This ruling was a disappointment for Dr Fenwick. He felt not enough weight was attached to the mitigating circumstances of Pearce's state of mind following his stroke. 'My own view was that section 37 was appropriate, but the defence wanted to go for a section 38 interim order probably because they knew the judge wouldn't accept a section 37.

'Pearce's dementia was accelerating. If you look up the mean length of life in somebody with vascular dementia it's about four years — this guy's only got about four years to live . . .

'If he'd gone to Broadmoor we'd have got better figures on his life expectancy, the way his dementia was affecting him and what caused him to get involved in crime. We could have also ensured that he took his medication.

'The problem he now faces is that he is going to find it very hard to survive in an ordinary prison environment. As a consequence of the frontal lobe damage, he is going to continue to display inappropriate behaviour. In prisons, you have to behave in a very specific way if you are going to survive. He, however, will behave in the way he feels appropriate, so he's at risk. He'll be beaten up in no time at all. He'll be rude to people, he'll insult inmates and he won't co-operate with prison staff.

'In my view Pearce had to be a suitable candidate for a hospital sentence and still is . . . If we'd had a hospital order then we could have allocated responsibility much more clearly in court than the judge was prepared to accept. The judge saw no medical factors. Edgar Pearce was just bad, but there are just so many medical factors they are dripping out of your ears.'

The one line of defence left to Nadine Radford had been dismissed. She'd have to make the best of what was left, which in truth was very little given the meagre time she'd had to prepare for the case.

In effect, she was going to have to throw Pearce before

the judge and beg for mercy. No-one fancied her chances very much.

Mrs Radford began by outlining Pearce's qualities. 'The defendant started life as a man who had great ambition and talent, a man who put himself through further education.' He had, she said, a promising career in advertising where he moved rapidly from position to position, always advancing himself. He did well for himself in that sphere. He later diversified into other skilled professions, including running a restaurant.

But, after his wife became ill and the restaurant was sold, things went downhill. And it all fell to pieces in 1992.

The stroke, his heavy drinking, his separation from his wife, his loneliness. Pearce had difficulty in dealing with ill people and therefore didn't or couldn't deal with his own problems. Also, after the stroke, Pearce was under the impression he had only two years to live.

But now came the really tricky bit. How could she mitigate in respect of his bombing campaign?

Her opening gambit was forthright. 'Mr Pearce does not hide behind the fact that he doesn't know the difference between right and wrong, although his interpretation may not be the same as most people.'

She outlined his inability to cope with the social consequences of his actions as he sunk into one-room isolation. 'Left alone, he had no feedback from anyone else about the decisions he was making. He believed he was practising his profession — running a public relations campaign to see if he could achieve his goal. He said although he did not regard money as the goal, he had to obtain the cards to get the money in order to win.'

Pearce had applied the principles of advertising to his campaign, 'To convince people of what you want to do by a plan that is consistent and persuasive.'

'In Mr Pearce's terms, left alone day in, day out he saw before him in fantasy and, in part, reality that other people had undertaken a scheme which had failed to achieve its goal and he had skills which could come to bear in this.'

Mrs Radford told Judge Hyam that Pearce had only wanted to see if he could complete the plan. The acquisition of the cash cards, not the money, was the prime objective.

This attempt to try and differentiate between the two was a last-chance tactic. But it was painfully tenuous. For most of the people in court, cards and cash were one and the same. This was mere semantics. A bomb is a bomb. Blackmail is blackmail no matter what the end objective. And a cash card is cash itself if you have the PIN number.

More glimpses of the pathetic state into which Pearce had descended were offered. The court heard how he had thought of his campaign as a form of personal contact between himself and his targets — he had even hoped there might be a special message on the screen of the cashpoint when he went to collect his money.

Of course Pearce's only real chance for mercy was his co-operation with the police following his arrest. His QC got straight to the point. 'By question six in his first police interview he had admitted being the Mardi Gra bomber and went on in great detail for page after page after page about why he did what he did. He was never intending in his own mind to cause injury to someone. He has pleaded guilty and accepted responsibility for these actions.' He was, she said, 'someone who was acting under a disability at the time.'

She finished by asking for credit to be given for Pearce's plea, his frankness with the police and for the time he had already served on remand to be taken into account. Also, given the doctor's prognosis of his reduced life expectancy due to advancing dementia, any time Pearce was to serve in prison would be a large part of what life he had left.

Mrs Radford threw one last thought to the court. 'If his illness had been recognised following his stroke and psychiatric treatment had been forthcoming, we might not all be here.'

There was little more she could say. Without the additional psychiatric evidence a referral to Broadmoor may have brought, what else was there to say? This was mitigation at its most difficult.

In the dock, Pearce began to stand. Judge Hyam waved him down with his hand. 'You can remain seated.'

Then he began.

'Edgar Pearce. You have pleaded guilty to the following offences . . .'

He reeled them off — blackmail, causing an explosion, actual bodily harm, unlawful possession of weapons. Pearce stared at the ground, his face expressionless.

'These offences were committed by you in the course of a campaign of extortion. Your apparent intention was to obtain a large amount of money first from Barclays Bank and then from Sainsbury's. Your plan was to terrorise the public, particularly staff and customers of Barclays and Sainsbury's by threats and by the planting of weapons designed to cause physical injury. Some of the devices which you used had the potential to cause death to anyone who was within range.'

Pearce's campaign had cost Barclays and Sainsbury's dear, said the judge. £140,000 in additional security for Barclays and an estimated £640,000 in lost business for Sainsbury's.

The injuries caused by Pearce's devices were read out — shock, muscular injuries, gunshot wounds. 'By good fortune alone,' said the judge, the potentially lethal devices did not kill anyone. 'Your motivations were greed and an insatiable appetite for notoriety. You paid no regard at all to the safety or well-being of the public at large who were constantly menaced by your activities.

'It has been said that blackmail offences are always serious and ugly. These offences were particularly serious, containing as they did, aggravating features. Your offences were planned with meticulous care, they were persistent and when you started to implement your demands by the use of weaponry you showed an ingenuity in making your devices progressively more dangerous and in sending them at random to members of the public. By placing them where members of the public would necessarily find them or be within range of them, you showed a cynical disregard of the feelings, physical and mental, of members of the community.

'Next, the sums of money which you were seeking were very substantial indeed and the cost to the public purse in bringing you to justice has been very large.

'Although a plea of guilty always goes some way to reduce the sentence which otherwise might have been passed, in your case because of the overwhelming evidence against you the reduction in your sentence for plea must be somewhat restricted. These offences were so serious that only a very substantial custodial sentence can be justified and only custodial sentences are adequate to protect the public from you. It is necessary, in addition to punish you for what you did, to impose exemplary sentences to deter others who might be minded to offend as you have done.'

The judge began to rattle off the sentences for each offence. 21 years, 21 years, 12 years, 12 years until he ran up a sentencing tally of 224 years in total. These individual sentences, said the judge, were to run concurrently, meaning Pearce would actually serve the length of the maximum sentence, 21 years.

Anyone who thought that now might be the time for Pearce to react in some way was to be disappointed. He remained as impassive as ever. He'd been expecting it.

Outside the Old Bailey, Jeffery Rees gave his reaction to the end of one of the most labour intensive investigations ever undertaken by a British police force. Surrounded by cameras and microphones he addressed the journalists. 'Edgar Pearce used as his model Rodney Whitchelo, the Heinz baby food extortionist. Like Whitchelo he has got a very long term of imprisonment. We hope that the message that goes out today is that extortionists, when they are caught, face very heavy penalties.'

Questions began to fire out of the surrounding pack. Was Mr Rees relieved the case was over? 'I'm very relieved considering where we were a year ago. Yes I'm very relieved.'

Did Pearce really pose that great a danger? 'I think he posed a very real danger, not just because of what he did but in terms of what was coming if he hadn't been caught when we did catch him.'

Will the sentence act as a deterrent to anyone else thinking about doing the same thing?

'I really do hope so, yes.'

What do you think of Edgar Pearce?

'I'm not going to answer that.'

What do you think of Edgar Pearce?

Burnt Wings

Welcome to the Mardi Gra Experience

What follows here is speculation, a personal view of why Edgar Eugene Pearce became one of Britain's most wanted men. This chapter is based on facts from the case, interviews carried out after Pearce's imprisonment and deductions drawn from what fragments are available of Pearce's life before he became the Mardi Gra Experience. Any opinions or conclusions are mine and mine only. I am not putting forward a theory that any one of the factors discussed below is responsible for making Pearce the man he became. What I am suggesting is that a complex cocktail of some or all of these factors have combined to create a man who, in certain circumstances, could turn into a man like Pearce.

To understand Edgar Pearce, we have to understand what in

itself he became. Pearce committed 36 almost identical crimes over a period of three years and three months. This repetitive, obsessive pattern of behaviour is highly indicative of the actions of a serial offender, someone who does not just commit crimes, but is *driven* to it.

Serial offenders are among the most intriguing and the most studied members of the criminal fraternity. Criminologists, psychologists, psychiatrists and detectives have spent years analysing their motives and actions in an attempt to find out what makes them tick. But the research is mainly concentrated one area — the serial killer. However, there are many other forms of serial offending.

And no matter what their crime — killer, rapist, stealer of women's underwear — the causes for serial offences have much common ground.

Serial offending finds its roots in fantasy. We all have fantasies and for many different reasons, but their end effect is usually the same — they make us feel better for a short while. The lonely man fantasies about the beautiful girlfriend he doesn't have; the single mother fantasises about the tranquil Greek island where she spent two blissfully quiet weeks the year before the twins were born; the road mender fantasises about what yacht he will buy when he wins the lottery and just where he'll stuff his spade when he goes to tell his boss he's quitting.

These fantasies are perfectly normal. Serial offenders use their fantasies, which may have been there since they were children, for the same reason. But their fantasies are based on much darker thoughts, thoughts which are the engine behind a compulsive cycle of behaviour. But a person doesn't become a serial offender until they've offended for the first time. This may sound like a truism, but there are millions of people who every day have moments of wild anger or frustration and fantasise about eliminating the cause of that anger or frustration. But 99.99999999% of us don't take that fantasy any further. However, a serial killer, for example, will continually fantasise about killing, becoming obsessed with that thought and only that thought. This constant focus on one unfulfilled desire begins to build tension. Over time, the tension increases and the only way to relieve it is to fantasise further. The fantasy then drives the nervous tension and the compulsion to kill builds up. The would-be killer may begin to act out parts of the fantasy, maybe beginning to trawl for a victim. The excitement this creates only serves to push the would-be killer on, until he realises he won't be sated until he completes the fantasy in reality.

In the aftermath of the offence, the tension inside the serial offender is released and the pressure they felt drops away. This is the stage where long gaps between offences are found. Because there is no tension, there is no offence. But with serial offenders, the tension will always return. It could be because they begin to feel guilty about what they have done or that the freshness the offending act brought to their minds begins to wear off. Either way the feelings of satisfaction they enjoyed after the offence fades and the compulsion returns, setting up a cycle of fantasy, tension, offence, calm, tension, fantasy, tension, offence that the serial offender cannot escape. The very act of first successful fantasy completion is their downfall because it sets up a further craving; they know the release that is attainable if they go all the way.

So how did Pearce end up in a pattern of offending? Until 1994, he was a law-abiding man, quietly trudging his way towards his pension. He drank too much; he had split from his wife; he was lonely. There are millions of men around the world who can tell the same story. His pattern of life consisted of a dozen small rituals; walking the half mile or so to his brother's house, walking to the pub, going to the supermarket, tinkering with his clocks. He lived an unremarkable, ordinary life. So what happened? Because, as Dr Peter Fenwick came back to time and again, something must have happened to turn this ordinary man into a notorious criminal. The useful handyman became a very useful bomber. Something happened.

That something is undoubtedly the 1992 stroke, but to just blame the stroke and the resulting brain damage is too simplistic. Judge Hyam clearly identified this as the central weakness in Pearce's application for a section 38 referral to Broadmoor. Hundreds of people suffer strokes and subsequent brain damage each year and hundreds of people develop dementia each year, yet this country is not overrun by hordes of demented, post-stroke criminals.

No, to try and understand why Pearce became the Mardi Gra bomber, we need to look deep into his life and examine who he is, what events and emotions shaped him and made him the man he was before 1992. Only then can we come close to seeing how he could step through the invisible boundary which holds us together, albeit loosely, as 'society' and into a no-man's-land where there are no rules and no responsibilities.

As we know, Edgar Eugene Pearce was the middle child of a traditional working-class family. Being a middle child is a unique familial position — a middle child usually exists in a kind of hierarchical vacuum. Many studies have shown that middle children view themselves as being in a 'lose-lose' situation — they neither enjoy the privileges traditionally enjoyed by the eldest child nor are they pampered as the youngest. More than that, they actually lose a social position when a third child comes along. The now middle child is usurped from its role as the family 'baby' and all the spoiling which accompanies that, and suddenly finds itself stuck between the elder child, who does everything first and gets everything first and the cosseted baby. This is what Pearce would have experienced with the birth of his young brother Philip.

Pearce's displacement within the family was to be augmented a few years later by his total transplantation out of the family. The young Pearce had stood out from an early age as being a bright child, so much so that it was felt local schooling was not sufficient for him. He won a place at a private school in Oxford and aged eleven was sent out of London to a new and strange life. The enormity of the opportunity afforded to him would have been a heavy weight to bear. On top of that, he had to bear it alone in Oxford, separated from his family foundations back in the East End. And while there may only be 50 or so miles between Leyton and Oxford, the true distance was cultural. The East End working-class boy was suddenly thrust into the comfortable privileges of middle-class Oxford society; the tailor's son found himself among a far more gilded crowd — the kind of people his father would have made clothes for. The pressure on him to squeeze the maximum possible value out of this opportunity must have been immense, whether exerted directly or indirectly — particularly as his schooling would have drained the family's modest coffers.

The three years Edgar spent at this school would have affected him immensely. He left his family and his culture to join a middle-class society he did not belong to and would not easily fit into. When he returned on holidays, he found that he no longer belonged to the East End. All the boys he used to play with had forged new relationships at their local school. More than that, they resented Edgar for going off to a 'posh' school and leaving them behind. So when Edgar returned home, it was no longer home, just a hostile landscape.

He put his nose to the grindstone and worked hard to make the best of his extraordinary opportunity. For three years he existed in limbo between the new world of private school and the old world of the East End. Then the rug was pulled out from under his feet. His father could no longer afford to send Edgar away. He had return to London and to the local state school. One of the reasons the family could no longer sustain Edgar's private education? The growing expense of looking after the new child, Philip.

Yet again, Edgar had lost out to the young usurper. And then, he had to accept the humiliation of having to face all his old friends at the school that 'wasn't good enough for him' three years ago.

Edgar's experiences were the seed for a pattern which later emerged in Pearce's adult life. Here we have a child who becomes used to things being continually taken from him, against a background of pressure to succeed and make the most of his intelligence, topped off with a feeling of isolation and never quite fitting in anywhere.

Years later we find a man who has the potential to succeed in whatever area he chooses to apply his skills. Yet, it never happens for him. Indeed, it tends to fall apart just as he about to achieve something substantial and worthwhile. What could lie underneath this? Was Pearce simply unlucky in life, or was he in some way shaping success into failure?

Ian Stephen is one of this country's most eminent psychologists. A chartered forensic psychologist and a chartered clinical psychologist, he has spent more than 30 years examining the motivations and the factors behind the lives of some of this country's most violent and disturbed criminals. An official spokesman for the British Psychological Society, his skills as a forensic psychologist have been called upon by three of top crime dramas — *Cracker*, *Prime Suspect* and *A Touch of Frost* — to help create authentic criminal characters.

Stephen says that in dealing with serial offenders like Pearce, first you have to identify the powerful mental processes that pattern their behaviour. These processes are called 'drivers'.

Stephen says that if an offender's driver can be identified, then their criminal behaviour can be more precisely explained.

If we look at Pearce's life history as outlined in Chapter Two, we can identify a pattern of success never quite attained. A promising career in advertising abandoned for a new life in South Africa; South Africa abandoned after six years and a return to England; a restaurant which never quite took off and had to be sold.

Stephen believes the root of Pearce's offending — his driver — could be related to his sense of failure; or rather his sense that he mustn't fail, but must live up to the potential he had shown since a young boy. He must be a success.

But the problem of trying to be successful is that first you have to run the risk of failure. People who have been successful in their chosen sphere have at some time failed. The key to their eventual triumph is having the resilience to come back and try again. But what if from day one that journey to success is weighed down by an overwhelming feeling that failure is not an option? This sets a different agenda for that journey. It stops being a journey to success. It's a journey to avoid failure.

Psychologists who have studied people with these kinds

of fears say the base of the fear is something that would have probably developed during childhood. If we apply this to Pearce, we can see the issues relating to his loss of familial position and the seesaw ride of his education as possible sources for such an anxiety. The displaced child who feels that he never fits in and has his 'golden opportunity' taken from him at a critical point in his development as a young adult; Pearce was withdrawn from private school aged fourteen, just as he would be preparing for the exams which would shape the rest of his life.

If, because of these experiences, Pearce developed a personality that centred on the avoidance of failure, rather than the achievement of success, we can start to explain how at 57 he became the Mardi Gra Experience.

A person whose driver is so powerful it leads them into crime is most likely to be classified as having a 'personality disorder'. Personality disorders are among the most controversial subjects in the legal and medical worlds. They have been labelled the 'dustbin' category for people who do not fit into society in some way. It is something that irritates and dismays Stephen. 'Under our legal system, he says, 'you are either mentally ill or your aren't mentally ill. If you are mentally ill and commit a crime, you go to a hospital like Broadmoor, otherwise its prison. There are a lot of people who fall between that and they are the groups of people now being labelled as having personality disorders. They simply go into the system, come out again and continue to commit offences, because they are never dealt with, merely contained. If they do end up in hospital, they are not treatable under the current provisions of the Mental Health Act, and are therefore labelled untreatable. In other words they don't respond to medication, they don't respond to normal therapies. It doesn't mean to say they can't respond to things, it's just that they can't respond to those things provided in a psychiatric hospital regime.'

A personality disorder is essentially an abnormal way of coping with the social environment in which a person exists. But someone with a personality disorder is not mentally ill. Stephen gives the following explanation. 'With a mental illness you're talking of something like a psychosis, where people hear voices, or a person thinks other people are telling them things or they have a paranoid delusional belief system where a person will hear the radio talking to them, or they will be watching television and think "this is about me". In these cases, a person's contact with reality is zilch.'

'Personality disorders operate on a slightly different level, because they are more to do with coping strategies. A person's contact with reality is quite good, but their interpretation of it may be different.

'Crudely, the difference between the two is this — someone hears a voice telling them to rob a garage as they pass it and they rob it. That's a psychotic system and that person is mentally ill. However, someone with a personality disorder will say: "I hate garages, so I'm going to rob them." '

'I had a patient who robbed bookies because as a child, his father spent all the family money gambling on horses. This patient wasn't psychotic. He had a good reality base, but the way he operated within it was not normal.'

When you're young, Stephen argues, new experiences and new difficulties crop up all the time. Children either learn to cope with them or they fail to learn to cope with them adequately. Taking Pearce as an example, if as a child he felt he had failed, his driver becomes: 'I must not fail'. He would then develop a technique or strategy for projecting the blame for any failures he may experience on anyone or anything that happens around him, so the blame never falls directly on him. In addition, people like this learn very skilfully to allow other people to make the decisions that make them a failure rather than the person making that decision themselves.

This overriding strategy to avoid failure is not a conscious process. It develops as a person learns how to cope with certain situations. However, this avoidant behaviour is not restricted to people who might be considered to be 'unsuccessful'. In his career, Stephen has come across a number of highly successful people who had reached the top of their professions, who nevertheless displayed various degrees of avoidant personality disorders. The great skill of these people was the ability to be able to put the blame for the outcome of a situation onto someone else. They were able to engineer scenarios to make sure someone else took the blame for an adverse outcome.

If we continue with the assumption that Pearce was driven by a need not to fail, then what proof is there to show that this need affected his life to such an extent that he developed an avoidant personality disorder? Well, let's take his life from the point at which he returned from the private school in Oxford. Here is a boy who has done something dramatic — particularly given the time, the late 1940s. Working-class boys from the East End did not go to private school, but by winning a place at one, Pearce had overcome the fairly rigid class structures that still operated in Britain at that time. And if he's managed to shatter the maxim that working-class boys don't go to private schools, then it was odds on that he was going to shatter the next no-no — that working-class children didn't go to universities, which in those days were almost entirely reserved for the children of middle and upper-class families. But Pearce never made it to university.

For reasons beyond his control he lost his private school tenure and returned to the working-classes. This was clearly not his fault. Yet he was still a bright lad, so he could still do well in his exams and make it to university. What does he do? He ends up at the local polytechnic (in those days considered entirely inferior to universities) taking what can be considered a vocational rather than an academic course — he is studying graphic design and advertising.

After completing his studies Pearce entered the advertising world and flourished, gaining 'promotion after promotion'. From what is known, it seems that these promotions occurred within smaller firms, based in London, the centre for the British advertising industry. So where's the avoidance? Well, it's not the job he's doing that's the problem, but where he's doing it. All of the firms he worked for were doubtless excellent firms, but they were not in the big league of advertising giants. And after more than a decade working his way through these smaller firms, Pearce does not emerge as any kind of shining star, simply a good, hard-working executive doing a good, solid job. He doesn't want to go for the big job with a prestigious firm because he's afraid he won't rise to the top in that high-pressure environment. Maybe it's better to be a large fish in a small pond. He can justify his lack of ambition by telling himself he hasn't been given the right opportunities, he didn't go to university, the top jobs are only open to a select cartel and so on. Just like Whitchelo, who blamed his failure to rise to the top of the police service on his not being invited to join the Freemasons.

The solution which presented itself as a means to rid himself of the middling career he had saddled himself with was to run away — to South Africa, to pursue a career as a 'freelance advisor' to a television film company. This can also be interpreted as an avoidance strategy, with Pearce starting a new life and a new job in a new country. But once in South Africa he again finds himself running with the pack, rather than leading it. The South Africa experiment is written off, with Pearce returning to England blaming the political situation for his return. Once back in the UK, he reinvents himself again, this time as a restaurateur. This phase is perhaps the most telling in Pearce's history in terms of pursuing the avoidant personality theory.

Jeanne's Cuisine was a small bistro in Hayling Island, an unremarkable, ordinary area of Hampshire. It is neither well-to-do nor run-down. It is perfectly average. Pearce bought the restaurant as a going concern and therefore it has to be assumed that it had a reasonable client base and turnover. Yet the restaurant didn't do well under Pearce. The suggestion is that his 'fancy' cooking didn't go down well with the locals, who preferred more conservative fare.

This smacks of a failure strategy. If a person cooks lavish food for diners who are not used to such food and do not like this sort of food, who is to blame? The obvious answer is Pearce, for not adapting his service to the local market. But, Pearce can say to himself that it is the fault of his customers — they simply don't appreciate good food. 'Pearls before swine', he can say. By trying to push back the boundaries of his customers' tastes, he is dooming himself to failure, but also setting up others to take the blame — his customers.

With the business ailing, Maureen falls seriously ill. Pearce admits he cannot cope and the restaurant has to be sold. The family return to London with just £5,000 to show for all their years of work. From here on in, it's all downhill for Pearce. A succession of nothing jobs combined with an increasing reliance on large quantities of alcohol to keep him going through the days. His marriage fails and Maureen moves out of their home. The bitterness at his failures in life grow during this time, as does his conviction that he has been done down by life in general. He blames them — anyone who never recognised his talents; a system which kept his bright light under a bushel. He drinks and broods; broods and drinks; then drinks some more.

His bitterness underpinned his vision of the world and his place in it. Then came 1992 and the stroke which would change his life forever. We know that following his stroke, a part of Pearce's brain was destroyed — which left him developing a failure to learn. On top of that, the specific area of Pearce's brain that was destroyed is the one that controls inhibitions. It stops people acting on impulse.

Stephen gives a real life example of this when telling the story of one of his patients. 'I had a patient once who was an absolutely brilliant maths academic. After being involved in a road accident he was frontally brain injured and subsequently went on to become sexually disinhibited, to the extent that while you were working with him he was constantly sticking his hand on your leg. Male or female, he was totally indiscriminate and quite aggressive under certain circumstances.

'While I was assessing him, the nursing staff would complain about his behaviour because they knew how intelligent he was and therefore could not see how someone so clever could not know it was wrong to do what he was doing. He would be told "stop touching me" and would stop. And then later he'd start touching people up all over again.'

Stephen suspected that the man's frontal lobe damage

had not only sexually disinhibited him, but also robbed him of the ability to recognise the moral consequences of what he was doing and to learn from them. To prove this, Stephen set an easy test. 'I gave the guy a maths test and he got top marks — and the nurses said "we told you, he's an intelligent man and he knows he is causing problems." I gave him the identical test the next day. The patient did it as though he'd never seen it before. The patient had retained his long-term functioning ability — his maths skills — but in terms of immediate learning he wasn't acquiring new skills. If your frontal lobes are damaged, the associations between past experience and current reality don't build up, so the person can be seen as having full faculties in terms of past knowledge and experience and may be able to work quite well in that context, but in terms of immediate morality and ideas of consequences — they are totally out of it.'

In Pearce's case, this inability to lean from his social environment was demonstrated during Dr Peter Fenwick's examinations. Pearce was unable to alter his approach to sorting out various shaped and coloured pieces of card, even when he was told time and again that he was doing it wrong. He just kept on going, unable to separate the immediate task of sorting from the stimuli around him that was telling him he should not be doing it that way.

If we assume that frontal damage played a part in Pearce's subsequent offending, things start to make sense. Here's a man who until a certain point in time displayed no signs of serious criminality. Yes, he could be unpleasant, but who isn't at some point? He never actually did anything serious. Before the accident, he was an angry man, but retained his natural inhibitions. He managed his frustrations through drinking, or taking it out indirectly by ranting at local children or at his neighbours when their dogs trespassed onto the front of his home. ('I'm going to poison them' he threatens, but never actually does anything). Then comes a catastrophic life event — serious brain injuries affecting the frontal lobes. With his ability to self-inhibit effectively knocked out, the latent malevolence inside him, which had hitherto been kept in check, was suddenly given the freedom to thrive. For Pearce, his hatred of the world which had denied him now defined him

This line of thinking does not seek to pin the blame for Pearce's offending solely on his brain damage. Pearce's brain injury was simply one ingredient in a potent cocktail.

Before his stroke, Pearce's resentment of the world at large — 'THEM' — was kept in check by a combination of his innate moral sense and alcohol. Now uninhibited, this hatred could surface for the first time.

Pearce is sat at home recuperating, ever more convinced that life has it in for him. During this time, he develops a concrete, child-like belief system — that 'THEY' have somehow prevented him from being a success. Then one day while watching television, he sees a programme about blackmail. In his uninhibted state, he sees blackmail as his route to success and revenge, without recognising the immorality of the crime.

But why does blackmail take his fancy? Why not robbing banks with a sawn off shotgun, or stealing cars, or breaking and entering?

Stephen's explanation is this, 'A person goes into Woolworths and fills a bag full of pick 'n' mix sweets. This person then goes to the counter to be served, but the assistants are chatting away to each other and ignoring the customer. There are three scenarios as a result. The person can say: "Excuse me, I'm waiting to get served would you mind finishing your conversation later" which is appropriate assertiveness, or they will start shouting and swearing at them, which displays short fuse anger, or they will stand there for ages being ignored, eventually put the sweets down and walk out of the shop. That night they go back to Woolworths and burn it down.

'Pearce fits into this last scenario, because most of these kinds of people are unable to assert themselves. They cannot confront a situation head on. Whereas most of us would say "excuse me", they will say nothing, so their anger level builds and doesn't get discharged until all of a sudden there is a sudden explosion.'

This model can be applied across many crimes and patterns of offending. To those people living around the evolving serial offender, outwardly there might appear to be nothing wrong. The surface will be calm and normal. Stephen says, 'It seems like nothing's happening. These are people you would describe as shy, quiet, wouldn't say boo to a goose; the perfect example is the two American boys from Colorado [Eric Harris and Dylan Klebold — see Chapter 4]. It is the shy ones you have to watch because they are ones that are going to blow. Look at Hungerford, look at Dunblane.' Stephen continues, 'I had a patient who committed the same crime three times, ten years apart. The build up involved him perceiving that his self-esteem was being damaged, but he would take it, it wouldn't upset him. It would take this particular latency period to a build up to a point where overflow comes and suddenly he would exhibit catastrophic behaviour. Some poor person would get on the end of it for something that was totally out of context with the situation they were in. People would say, "he's getting upset over nothing.' But it's that one thing that eventually triggers the explosion because there was a whole history of build up.'

Pearce's sudden explosion seems to have resulted from the release of years of pent-up resentment facilitated by his brain damage. And his explosion took the form of bombs. We can't know what made him chose a bombing campaign, other than to guess he probably drew on his past knowledge of firearms. But his choice betrays his inability to confront situations head on. He feels comfortable with remote violence.

The descent into serial offending brings with it a change in lifestyle the offender is probably not aware of until they are well progressed along their new journey. Once it's started, it's almost impossible to stop without professional help. This is because the aim of the serial offender is not necessarily to achieve completion of the crime itself, but to achieve perfection in perpetrating that crime. Consider Nadine Radford's mitigation statement, 'He believed he was practising his profession — running a public relations campaign to see if he could achieve his goal. He said although he did not regard money as the goal, he had to obtain the cards to get the money in order to win.'

Pearce had to win, on his own terms. And once he had decided that getting cash cards from Barclays and later Sainsbury's was the way, he had to have them. He was compelled to. If you look at the pattern of Peace's bombing, there are great hot spots of activity interspersed with prolonged fallow periods. He tries to achieve success at blackmail and fails, so he stops. But he is drawn back to blackmail time and time again. He has to get those cards. He has to win. And when he finally forced Sainsbury's to print the cards, he doesn't get just one — which would have been sufficient to access the money.

He collects 10. They were his trophies.

Stephen describes similar compulsive behaviour in a

patient who was a serial burglar who 'literally could not go to sleep unless he had burgled a house before. What he stole was irrelevant, he didn't need it. It was the process of breaking into the house, the excitement that drove him.'

Pearce's blackmail campaign also served another purpose in his post-stroke life. After his discharge from hospital, his mind must have been in turmoil. His failed marriage, no job, no prospect of work, no money, pain from his broken shoulder, his alcoholism. He needed to focus on something. His blackmail plan gave him function, a role in life, an identity, elevating him to a position he had longed for all his life — to be one step ahead of the herd. He was probably telling the truth when he said the money wasn't the issue. It was what led to it that became important.

A good parallel is the compulsive gambler, where the process of gambling is as meaningful as the result. So for Pearce, the preparation for a bomb attack was probably as significant as the bombing itself. There would be the excitement in preparing the bomb, sourcing the various components, choosing a location, sending demands, and finally planting the device. And look at the care he took in making his devices — up to three days — and his continual change of design and placement reveals there was more going on than a simple campaign of consumer terrorism. His bomb making was his art.

It would be easy to dismiss everything that has been said so far in this chapter as spurious psychological excuses. The prosecution went for the jugular: Pearce was greedy man who didn't care that he might kill people. A ruthless, calculating man who meticulously planned every detail of a concerted blackmail campaign.

Pearce was a crook — plain and simple.

Except that it's never that simple.

Peace was the blackmailer who . . .

• Cleverly chose only random targets to fool the police — yet he only bombed on his own doorstep.

• Set out to perfect Rodney Whitchelo's blackmail plan — but made exactly the same mistake.

• Planted bombs in shopping bags and crowded public places — but is offended at the suggestion he set out to hurt people.

• Stops a bombing campaign not because people were getting hurt, but because he thought some Barclays staff might lose their jobs.

• Set out to collect his blackmail money in a disguise so ludicrous it guaranteed everyone noticed him.

• Collected his money in the same locations he had previously bombed.

• Was a loner — who took his brother along to witness the end stage of his crime.

It doesn't make sense. Unless you take on board at least some of the 'spurious' psychology.

The tight bombing range Pearce operated within was one of the most characteristic — and baffling — aspects of the case. The police brought in a geographic profiler to try and solve the riddle, but to no avail. The bombing centres of west and south east London stuck out like a sore thumb. Nearly everybody had correctly deduced the bomber lived in west London. But the south east attacks had everyone guessing. What was the connection? The answer was revealed by Pearce after his capture; the south east targets were chosen because they were in the area of his estranged wife's new home. But that doesn't answer why only those areas were targeted. The reason is Pearce's brain damage. Dr

Peter Fenwick's prison tests revealed how the destruction of part of Pearce's left frontal lobe had robbed him of the ability to adapt to new situations and Ian Stephen's experience with the maths expert show how this kind of damage can limit a person's perceptual base to that which existed at the point the brain damage was incurred.

Pearce's perceptual base was fixed in west and south east London. So that's where he bombed. He was unable to think past this boundary, couldn't recognise the inherent risk of bombing on his own doorstep. This limitation on his knowledge is also reflected in his bomb-making skills. Pearce was able to make his devices thanks to his previous knowledge of firearms learnt in South Africa. But although he was forever tinkering with his methods, perfecting an art as he saw it, the bombs never developed in their sophistication. Success or failure, essentially the same explosive method was used again and again.

And the same reason lies behind Pearce's bizarre decision to collect his money from locations he had previously bombed. He can't 'see' beyond the page of the map that exists in his mind.

The other thing he can't see beyond is his goal. Pearce's plan was to target rich, sensitive institutions. But he was blinked. What he didn't see was that by targeting institutions (with bombs) he was in fact targeting people. Other people were irrelevant to him. He doesn't know them, so they aren't real. When people got hurt, he blamed the institutions. It would have been their fault for either not finding the bombs in time or for not capitulating. ('*My aim was for security staff to be on their toes and collect them. Injuries simply weren't necessary.*')

Yet this attitude is totally contradicted by his stated reasons for ending the campaign at Barclays — because he's afraid that people will lose their jobs. Here, he demonstrates a clear understanding of the consequences of his actions. How can these contradictions be reconciled?

Pearce has always thought of himself as the unrecognised worker. He empathised with the 'little people' who were at the mercy of the bosses. He drew on his past experience. He didn't want anyone to have to go through what happened to him. Losing your job equals failure. He targeted the organisations as entities. It's the entity bit that's more important as he is managing to do things to the 'people' that have done things to him.'

Another important element in Pearce's makeup is power. If success equals power, then power was something he felt he had been denied all his life. By choosing blackmail, Pearce placed himself in a position of huge power. By embellishing his campaign with a demonstrated willingness to strike at random targets, he increased the power he had.

He forced Barclays and then Sainsbury's to recognise this by saying, 'I can pick anybody'. He also knew how much time the authorities would spend trying to connect his targets and by watching all those people and all those millions of pounds get diverted, he felt ever more powerful.

These power games continued even after Pearce was caught and was being interviewed. He gave an immediate and full confession and by doing so took control of where things were going. Being under arrest and in police custody is about as controlled an environment it is possible to be in. The police like to be in control and to collect the evidence (including a confession) against the prisoner in a set way. Yet it is Pearce who sets the agenda for evidence discovery and by doing so is he is able to establish a little platform for himself. This is important to him because he knows the police have gone to his house and he knows what they'll find. Pearce didn't want to be presented with evidence and asked to explain. He wanted to deliver it himself. The fact he was telling the police everything prevented them from using the evidence against him.

Perversely, the fact that Pearce had been caught also validated him in his own eyes. For much of his campaign, Pearce had been blacked out, prevented from entering the public's consciousness. How infuriating for him: ignored again even though he was finally doing something. It was never going to be enough for his targets and the police to know. People had to know because how was anyone ever going to realise how clever he was unless they knew who was doing it? This was achievable in the first instance by the use of the snappy Mardi Gra logo and image. This branding solved a key problem for Pearce — gaining an identity without being identified. The whole point of any criminal exercise where capitulation is the intended result is that the meaning of the exercise is lost unless someone or something can be labelled as being the perpetrator (take terrorist bombings as another example). The perpetrator has to be able to claim responsibility to show their power. By the end, Pearce wasn't satisfied with the success of making Mardi Gra a household name. He wanted personally to be recognised for it.

He was the Mardi Gra Experience.

Maybe that need for recognition made him repeat the mistakes he had set out to avoid. From the start he was trying to supersede Rodney Whitchelo as the blackmailer par excellence. Yet he was captured in exactly the same way — by observation of cashpoint machines. Why did he repeat Whitchelo's mistake if he was trying to improve on his campaign? He wanted to choose the same method to actually prove he could do it, while Whitchelo, the policeman, couldn't. What he didn't pick up though, was the fact that the method itself was flawed, rather than the person. Pearce would have assumed Whitchelo failed because of some inadequacy. Pearce in fact came no way near surpassing Whitchelo, in sophistication of approach to the targets or in the collection of money itself. Whitchelo criss-crossed the country, doing everything he could to avoid detection. Pearce simply lumbered into the areas he had previously bombed. If the aim was to improve Whitchelo's method, why ape it in such a crass way? The answer could be the well-documented phenomenon of perpetrators being drawn back to the scenes of the crimes. Serial offenders get caught in ever-decreasing circles of offending which usually lead to their capture. Interviewed after being caught, many serial killers have said that it was as though they had a need to be caught, that they were unconsciously creating mistakes that would lead to capture because capture created an irreversible break in the cycle of offending. If that is true for serial killers, then why not serial a serial bomber/blackmailer?

Captured alongside Pearce on April 28 was his brother Ronald, who was observed accompanying Edgar at a number of cashpoints on the day of arrest. Apart from asking the question 'why on earth did Ronald meekly stand alongside his brother as he withdrew the proceeds of Britain's most notorious blackmail?' we can also ask why on earth did Edgar take Ronald along?' In his police interview, all Edgar would says was, 'My brother was with me because it took three to four years for me to get to this position and I was elated. I wanted to show him some real magic.'

I wanted to show him some magic.

All his life, Edgar had felt expectation on his shoulders

and had failed to live up to that expectation. Ronald had followed in his father's footsteps. Edgar had struck out and had got his wings burnt and had to endure the humiliation of trying to reach above his station only to come crashing down. Ronald was a stable character, someone who didn't set the world on fire. He had an ordinary job, a small ordinary flat, a nice stable relationship.

He was everything Edgar wasn't. He was everything Edgar wanted to be.

Because he was free.

Normality. No pressure to succeed. No failure. You can't be frustrated if you don't have ambition. If you've never taken a risk, you can't taste failure. But this moment — this withdrawal of cash — was Pearce's success, his crowning moment. For a while he had beaten the system, he had beaten THEM and he wanted people to know about it.

Edgar was like a child with a new bike, showing off.

Look what I can do. Look at me. I'm a success.

At last I'm a success.

Edgar Pearce became the Mardi Gra bomber because he didn't want to spend the rest of his life stuck in a small room, destined never to realise the potential he knew he possessed and which he believed had been frustrated for reasons that were completely beyond his control

It is perhaps ironic that is exactly what he is now condemned to do. His cell in HMP Belmarsh is smaller than his room at 12, Cambridge Road North. Only, sitting in his cell he has no red wine to take away the loneliness, no television to soak up the endless hours waiting for something, anything, to happen.

Edgar Pearce now has only his dreams of what could

have been and the certain knowledge that he will now never get the chance to become what he always wanted to be — a success.

Because of his medical condition he will probably die in prison.

'There is no old age for a man's anger. Only death.'
Sophocles